"A POWERFUL STORY"
—*The Baltimore Sun*

"A fine memoir of Aranka Siegal's childhood in Hungary . . . you feel the power and interest of her particular experience and remember that this story cannot be told too often" —*Newsweek*

"STUNNING . . . DRAMATIC AND MOVING . . . a touching addition, effective and affective, to the growing body of books about the Holocaust"
—*Bulletin of the Center for Children's Books*

"A bit of history at its best" —*VOYA*

"Powerful . . . heartrending . . . Piri's point of view adds poignancy to an account of one of the great tragedies of all time" —*Horn Book*

"UNFORGETTABLE . . . POIGNANT . . . DRAMATIC . . . mirrors the tragedy of Jews in the occupied countries" —*ALA Booklist*

"A moving and graphic portrayal of the closeness and hope of people bound together in a terrible time"
—*McNaughton Book Service*

UPON THE HEAD
OF THE GOAT

Stories of Courage from SIGNET and SIGNET VISTA

☐ **MOTTELE by Gertrude Samuels.** He was only twelve but World War II had stolen his childhood. A true-life novel "of Jews who *did* fight back . . . vital . . . alive . . . well worth reading."—Stephen Longstreet (075234—$1.75)

☐ **STOLEN YEARS by Sara Zyskind.** Sara Plager was eleven when the Nazis invaded Poland. She was a young woman of seventeen when their reign of horror ended. This is the story of those six years—that should have been full of joyful discovery, but instead were filled with savage suffering and supreme testing. (120116—$3.50)*

☐ **UPON THE HEAD OF THE GOAT: A Childhood in Hungary 1939–1944 by Aranka Siegal.** Based on the author's own childhood experiences, the story of nine-year-old Piri Davidowitz and her family is that of countless Jews in Europe during World War II. It is a story of the many who were lost and of the few with the luck and the courage to survive. "Brings the truth home about a time that we must neither forget nor deny"—*Philadelphia Inquirer.* (120841—$2.25)*

☐ **CHILD OF THE HOLOCAUST by Jack Kuper.** They had taken his family away, and now they were after him. . . This is the stirring true story of how one little boy, Jakob Kuperblum, alone and afraid, survived in a world of misery and hopelessness controlled by the Nazis. ". . . Bears comparison to *The Diary of Anne Frank* and *The Painted Bird*."—Publishers Weekly (112482—$2.50)

☐ **CHERNOWITZ! by Fran Arrick.** Ninth grader Bobby Cherno could handle a bully—but anti-semitism was something else . . . "A frightening reminder that the spread of racial prejudice can happen anywhere."—*Horn Book* (122860—$2.25)*

*Prices slightly higher in Canada

Buy them at your local bookstore or use this convenient coupon for ordering.
THE NEW AMERICAN LIBRARY, INC.,
P.O. Box 999, Bergenfield, New Jersey 07621
Please send me the books I have checked above I am enclosing $_____
(please add $1.00 to this order to cover postage and handling) Send check or money order—no cash or C.O.D.'s Prices and numbers are subject to change without notice
Name_____
Address_____
City _____ State _____ Zip Code _____
Allow 4-6 weeks for delivery
This offer is subject to withdrawal without notice

UPON THE HEAD OF THE GOAT

A CHILDHOOD IN HUNGARY
1939-1944

ARANKA SIEGAL

A SIGNET VISTA BOOK

NEW AMERICAN LIBRARY

NAL BOOKS ARE AVAILABLE AT QUANTITY DISCOUNTS
WHEN USED TO PROMOTE PRODUCTS OR SERVICES
FOR INFORMATION PLEASE WRITE TO PREMIUM MARKETING DIVISION,
NEW AMERICAN LIBRARY, 1633 BROADWAY,
NEW YORK, NEW YORK 10019.

RL 6/IL 5+

This is an authorized reprinte of a hardcover edition published by
Farrar, Straus & Giroux, Inc. The hardcover edition was published
simultaneously in Canada by McGraw-Hill Ryerson Ltd., Toronto

SIGNET VISTA TRADEMARK REG U S PAT OFF AND FOREIGN COUNTRIES
REGISTERED TRADEMARK—MARCA REGISTRADA
HECHO EN CHICAGO, U S A

SIGNET, SIGNET CLASSIC, MENTOR, PLUME, MERIDIAN AND NAL BOOKS
are published by New American Library,
1633 Broadway, New York, New York 10019

First Signet Vista Printing, February, 1983

3 4 5 6 7 8 9 10 11

PRINTED IN THE UNITED STATES OF AMERICA

*This book is dedicated to
those who did not survive. They are
deathless and timeless. Auschwitz could not
sever the bonds of love and friendship
which contributed to my survival and which
will live within me to the end of my days.*

And the Lord said unto Moses ". . . Aaron shall lay both his hands upon the head of the live goat, and confess over him all the iniquities of the children of Israel, and all their transgressions, even all their sins; and he shall put them upon the head of the goat, and shall send him away by the hand of an appointed man into the wilderness."

LEVITICUS 16

KOMJATY

1

From the time I was five my mother would send me from Beregszász to spend the summers with my grandparents in Komjaty. The open fields, the river, and the forest of this Ukrainian village became my playground. The color of the wild flowers, the feel of the forest, the sound of the water, the humming of the insects, the warmth of the animals—those experiences became the play from which I learned so much.

I rose to the rooster's crowing and roamed everywhere until dusk. What seemed strange at first—the people, their clothes and habits—quickly became familiar. Their language was Ukrainian, but Babi spoke to me in Yiddish. "No, not Hungarian, or Ukrainian," said Babi; "you must learn Yiddish." Soon I could ask questions in three languages.

In 1939, when I was nine, the impending war in the rest of Europe still seemed far away from us and my mother had sent me to Komjaty to spend the spring holidays with Babi and my older sister Rozsi. Mother, not wanting Babi to live by herself after the death of Grandpa Rosner, had decided to send each one of us five girls in turn to stay with Babi. She started with Lilli, the oldest. Lilli, however, did not last long as Babi's companion. She met her husband, Lajos, in Komjaty and, after a summer romance, was married at sixteen. Then it was Rozsi's turn to join Babi.

Like Babi, Rozsi thrived on the farm. She shared Babi's love for the animals and the fertility of the fields. Life in Komjaty was predictable and simple. The climate and the seasons made the decisions for the inhabitants. At twelve years of age, Rozsi knew that she wanted to live with the land. She wanted earth, not cement, under her feet.

A few days after I arrived, a major battle over disputed borders broke out between Hungary and the Ukrainian Resistance Fighters trying to hold on to their independent state. Babi, Rozsi, and I could hear bursts of gunfire from the border most of the day. The women, children, and old people huddled together in their small whitewashed and straw-thatched houses. The animals had been gathered and locked in the barns. Babi sat in her chair in the kitchen, with her shawl around her, fingering the worn pages of her prayer book as her mouth moved in silent prayer. Rozsi sat beside her, crocheting.

I was frightened and cried, wishing I were home in the safety of my own city in Hungary. Babi's house seemed small and exposed, set in the midst of her flat fields. The fence around it was only waist-high and the gates were without locks. The front porch didn't have a gate and led right to the kitchen entrance. The kitchen was the center of the house, flanked on each side by a bedroom. The larger of these served as dining and sitting room, as well as our bedroom. The guest bedroom on the other side was used mainly for storage. None of the rooms seemed very secure to me; anyone could easily enter any time.

"I want to go home," I said.

"Don't be afraid," comforted Babi. "Nothing bad will come to us. Our house is full of His books, and they will protect us."

I was not completely reassured when, toward the end of the day, I heard a rowdy bunch of victorious Hungarians march up the road. I ran out with my long, knotted scarf of red, white, and green and tied it to Babi's gatepost as a welcome sign. The village was kept awake long into the night with the sounds of celebration coming from the tavern.

Babi lit the kerosene lamp and let it burn until I fell asleep. In the morning when I awoke, I immediately went over to the window and looked out: I was curious to see if Komjaty had changed overnight under the Hungarian occupation. Dressing quickly, I went into the kitchen, looking for Babi and Rozsi, but they were in the barn, tending the animals.

I put on my sheepskin coat and red rubber boots and went out into the woods. The forest ground was a patchwork of colorful flowers, gray puddles, and white snow. By the time I had gathered a bouquet of flowers, my cotton stockings were soaked with icy water, and I realized that my boots had several small holes in them.

As I started to run back to Babi's house, I could hear the loud gushing of the river and went to look at it. All the lesser streams, as well as the melting snows, channeled into the Rika at this time of year, swelling the water so that it rushed down, taking away everything lying in its path except the largest boulders.

My attention was caught by a log floating toward me. As the current carried it closer, I realized that it was not a log but a body. It was a body clad in a Ukrainian uniform, face up, approaching head first. Despite my uneasy confusion, I stepped closer to the water's edge and stooped on a rock to get a better look. The face, puffy with death, was that of a boy between eighteen and twenty. He had the high cheekbones so typical of the young men of Komjaty, but I couldn't tell whether his eyes were open or closed. I dropped my crocuses, and soon they were floating, scattered on that young man's body as the stream flowed past me.

I saw two more soldiers in the river before I turned my back. These bodies, in the middle of the river, were being thrown from rock to rock. The bodies all had one thing in common; they were all missing hats and boots. Thinking of my stepfather, whom I had so often seen in his officer's uniform, and of my baby brother, Sandor, who would grow up to wear one, I started running again and did not stop until I reached Babi's warm kitchen.

Babi was standing in the doorway putting on her shawl, getting ready to go out to look for me. "Don't you know better than to run off without telling us where you're going?" she scolded with concern in her voice.

"But, Babi, I saw three dead men floating in the Rika!" I said. She didn't say another word, but took off her shawl, wrapped it around me, and walked us back into the kitchen while I continued, "They were Ukrainian soldiers. What will become of them?"

Without answering, Babi gently guided me down into the chair, took off my wet boots and stockings, fixed hot milk, and cut a thick slice of black bread which she buttered and sprinkled with coarse sugar. As I drank the milk and ate the sweet, crunchy bread, I watched the burning logs turn to ashes in the open stove while Babi carefully worked the thread through her loom. Her voice came toward me from what seemed a great distance, although she was not more than two meters away. "They are at peace now," she said, as she worked her loom. Soon I fell asleep and did not awaken until Rozsi returned from her day in the fields.

There were no more reprisals by the Ukrainians, and a few days after seeing the bodies in the river I went into the fields, where the villagers were trying to make up for lost time. Because of the fighting, they had been afraid to go out to farm the fields. I watched them work for a while, and had just started toward the river when I heard the metallic sound of hoofs hitting the rocks in the dirt road. Horses were rare in Komjaty; most of the wagons were pulled by oxen and few people in the village kept horses.

Surprised, I turned to see a Hungarian mounted policeman—even more of a rarity in Komjaty. He was dressed in the traditional Hungarian uniform of gray-green flannel, fastened by rows of brass buttons and trimmed in braid. His hard-crowned hat was topped by long black and green feathers from a rooster's tail, and the hat was held in place by a narrow black leather strap encircling the young man's clean-shaven chin. He waited for my eyes to meet his before he broke the silence. "Am I on the right road for Komjaty?"

"There is only one road," I said.

"I am coming from Salánk," said the policeman, "and I have to get back before dark. I was told it was four kilometers."

"You must be heading for Big Komjaty," I said, "because Little Komjaty is just beyond the clearing." I pointed the way. "Can you see it from up there?" I was no taller than the horse's legs.

"I was told that people here don't speak Hungarian."

"That is true, but I am from Beregszász, and I am here on vacation visiting my grandmother."

"Where does your grandmother live?"

"Just up the road—the sixth house on the left."

"Would you like a ride back?" he asked, getting off the horse. Before I had time to answer, his gloved hands gripped my waist and lifted me up the height of the giant horse. He mounted behind me, and resting up against his chest, I could feel his brass buttons and belt buckle through my light cotton dress. He asked me my name, and I told him in a breathless voice, "Piri Davidowitz." I was overcome with the thrill and pride of sitting up so high, and anticipated relating the whole experience to my friend Molcha.

Babi, along with a group of villagers, was in the road, watching in awe the unaccustomed sight of a mounted policeman. The scene had created almost as much excitement in Komjaty as the appearance of the first car in Beregszász.

"Is everything all right?" Babi managed to ask in Hungarian.

"Oh, yes, your granddaughter was giving me directions to the police headquarters in Big Komjaty. I am on official business from Salánk. She also told me that she is on a visit from Beregszász. I don't know if you are aware of it, but the borders are temporarily closed and the trains are not running. Piri's vacation may last longer than you planned."

Babi took in this information very slowly and then replied, "May this be the worst the war brings us. Would you like to have a cool drink of water before riding on?"

He got off the horse, lifted me down, and set me next to Babi. Removing his helmet, he saluted her, clicking together the heels of his boots. "My name is Wajda, Ferenc," he announced and then added, "Yes, thank you, I would like some water."

Babi went into the kitchen and returned with one of her

good glasses filled with cold water. She handed it to Ference, who drank it down in a few gulps and gave the glass back to her.

"Your granddaughter is quite a little lady; I was lucky to meet someone who speaks Hungarian."

Babi nodded. "My name is Rosner, Fage."

Ferenc replaced the heavy helmet on his head and mounted his horse. After he left, the villagers walked away, without comment. Frowning with distrust, Babi took my hand and led me into the house.

2

Several weeks later, I was on the porch when I spotted Ferenc in the distance. He stopped at our gate, and I was flattered that he remembered me when I ran up to him.

"*Szervusz,* Piri," he greeted me. "Would it be all right with your grandmother if my horse and I had some water?"

"Grandma is out in the fields, but I think it would be all right for me to give you some water." Inside me, I was not certain at all; I had a strange feeling about him and Babi. I could not explain it, but he did not seem to fit in with her life. Babi took up so little space while he needed so much. I felt he could crush her in some way. I tried to hide my fear.

"Are you coming on official business again?"

"Oh yes, I will have to make this trip regularly."

"What does official business mean?"

"I deliver the new rules from the new government."

Taking the water bucket from the kitchen, I ran across the road to our neighbor's well while Ferenc led his horse to the trough. Tercsa's water, clearer than Babi's, came from a mountain spring. As I drew the water bucket up from the well, I looked over into our yard to see Ferenc standing in the shade of one of Babi's plum trees. He seemed large and rigid under the umbrella of white blossoms. As if reading my thoughts, he suddenly removed his helmet and shook the feathers free of petals. Without his helmet, he looked much younger and more human. He had a handsome face, but his mouth and chin were soft, like a girl's. I finished drawing the water and returned to our yard, carrying the full bucket. Ferenc took a cupful and asked, "Don't you get lonesome here without friends?"

"I usually come here with my sister Iboya to help Rozsi, but Iboya was sick so I came without her. Then the trains stopped running and she couldn't join me."

"Has your grandma always lived here?"

"Always."

"Then how come she can speak Hungarian?"

"From visits to us in Beregszász." Again that uneasy feeling about Ferenc and Babi crept up in my stomach. I stopped talking.

"Who is Rozsi?"

"She is my older sister—she is in the fields with my grandmother."

When the horse had finished drinking, Ferenc saluted me again and rode off.

A few months later, Rozsi was picking some snapdragons near the fence for our Sabbath table. She was singing as she worked, absorbed in the task, when Ferenc appeared on the road. All motions and song stopped at once; I could see Rozsi's stunned face from the porch where I was peeling potatoes. Ferenc came up to our gate and dismounted. Taking off his helmet, he bowed gallantly in greeting.

"My name is Wajda, Ferenc; I am an acquaintance of your sister Piri."

Rozsi remained speechless. I came up to her. "Ferenc is the policeman I told you about."

"And you must be Rozsika," said Ferenc, adding the endearment—*ka*.

There was a long, silent pause as Ferenc and his horse continued to stand outside the gate while Rozsi and I remained inside. Finally, Rozsi found her voice and said, "You may water your horse here if you like."

"I'll run and fetch water from Tercsa's well," I volunteered and went to get the water bucket.

When I returned, Rozsi was standing by the trough near Ferenc. She held the yellow flowers in her right hand and stroked the horse with her left. Ferenc was watching her and hardly noticed me when I offered him the water. Rozsi was wearing her holiday dress; its bodice hugged her small chest while the full skirt billowed out from her waist to her slim ankles. Holding her head high, she looked over the horse at Ferenc, and her long, chestnut-brown hair glistened in the sunlight.

They were talking about the effects of the Hungarian occupation on Komjaty. "These people will never learn Hungarian," Rozsi was saying. "They are Ukrainian and they will always be Ukrainian. There is little room for politics or learning new things in their lives. Their time is taken up just by surviving."

"What about you?" Ferenc asked. "Aren't you bored by this simple life? Don't you miss the cinema in the city?"

"Not really . . ." Rozsi started to answer when Babi came walking through the fields beyond the back of the house. We saw her stop, put her hand over her eyes to shield out the midday sun, and then take the roundabout way to the house through the vegetable garden. It was obvious that she did not want to confront our visitor, and we sensed her annoyance. Rozsi stopped stroking the horse. Ferenc handed me back the cup, took up the bridle of his horse, and led him to the gate.

"Would it be all right for me to stop again?" he asked hesitantly.

Playing with her flowers, Rozsi answered slowly, "Yes, I think so." Ferenc mounted his horse, turning back once before he disappeared out of sight.

As we entered the house, Rozsi and I exchanged looks of apprehension. Babi was in the kitchen, cutting up turnips, and when she noticed us, her knife came down hard on the cutting board. Rozsi picked up a vase from the cupboard and began to arrange the flowers in it. Babi scraped the turnips into a pot, added water, and put it on the hot stove. Then she exploded.

"That was a fine picture I just witnessed on my land. If

you live long enough, you see everything. I can understand Piri's befriending one of them, but you, Rozsi, I'm disappointed. I thought you were old enough to know better."

"We were only giving him water," I said.

"My granddaughters do not have to slake the thirst of our enemy. I had no choice the day he brought you back from the Rika, but Rozsi doesn't have to pay attention to him."

"Just because he is Hungarian doesn't mean that he is an enemy," protested Rozsi, her face flushed. I felt sorry for her; this was the first time I ever heard Babi speak to Rozsi in anger. I sat down on one of the kitchen stools.

Babi began to speak again in a calmer voice. "Rozsi, don't you know that the Hungarians have been our enemies for years? Since the World War they have been against Jews. We were blamed for the loss of their territories, and for hard times. Everything that went wrong was our fault. They came tearing through here with their pogroms, wanting to kill every Jew. We were not safe in our houses; we were even afraid to go to sleep. That is why three of my children ran off to America."

"But that was under Béla Kun. Now Horthy is head of state for Hungary, and he is a friend of the Jews," said Rozsi.

"No, Rozsi. As long as there are wars they will always need scapegoats, and as long as we are here, we will be chosen."

Rozsi stopped setting the table and went outside. Babi sat down next to me. She started to stroke my hair, and I realized that I had been crying. When she spoke her voice was soft. "I should have told you all this before, Piri, but I was hoping that your generation would be spared. A Jew always hopes; it is his nature. But I am afraid that we now have another madman, that Hitler stirring up all of Europe. He marches over others' lands like a plague. He is looking to take all of Europe for Germany. He takes from the Czechs with one hand and gives it away to the Hungarians with the other. But he doesn't give anything away for nothing. He is buying the Hungarian army for himself with that land. And they've already started taking jobs away from the Jews. That's today, and tomorrow, who knows?''

''Where is he now?'' I asked, my voice wavering as I pictured this monster man moving across the fields with arms as long as the telephone poles in Beregszász.

''In Poland,'' said Babi. She got up and walked over to the stove, to continue her dinner preparations. I was comforted by the distance of Hitler from us, but my mind whirled in the confusion of trying to understand all the things Babi had said to Rozsi and me—pogroms, scapegoats—was this what being a Jew meant?

Somewhere in my heart I had known that my Christian friends were different from me; that I lived in their world, not they in mine; that laws came from their world, not mine; that school closed for Christmas and Easter, not Hanukkah and Passover. I had accepted these rules without thinking much about them, just as I accepted having to wash my face and brush my hair. The code was part of my awareness, but I did not dwell on it.

In Beregszász I went to public school and did not choose my friends or separate them by religion. On our street lived Hungarian, Czechoslovak, Russian, and Jewish families. My mother was friendly with all of them. I had attended Protestant services with Ica Molnar and Orthodox Russian services with Vali and Milush Veligan, and Mother did not seem to mind when I had told her where I was going.

But Babi's attitude toward the Hungarians was not like Mother's. I remembered an incident that took place during the summer of Grandpa Rosner's death, when Babi was still wearing black clothes and staying in the house, reading her prayer book. I spent more and more time playing outside with the children of Komjaty. One day as we passed one of the corner shrines, all the other children stopped, bowed, made a cross over their chests, and said a prayer in Ukrainian. Their movements impressed me; I watched their gestures and then imitated them, bowing and making a cross over my chest. Later, when I got home, Babi took me into her bedroom and closed the door. She was very angry. "Somebody told me you made a cross over yourself. Is that true?"

"No, I didn't do it, the others did."

She picked me up and stood me on a chair so that she could look into my eyes as she faced me. "Now, look into my face. Did you make a cross over yourself, or did this person tell me a lie?"

"I made a cross over myself."

"Don't you know you're Jewish?"

"Yes, Babi."

"Yes, what?"

"Yes, I'm sorry."

"If you don't have respect for your religion, how do you expect others to?"

I respected my religion, but it was hard for me to think of all those people so much a part of my life in Beregszász as enemies. The Ukrainian farmers of Komjaty seemed far more unfriendly than the Hungarians I knew.

Babi was still busy at the stove, so I asked, "What about the Christians here, the farmers, do they like the Jews?"

She turned to face me as she answered my question. "They concern themselves more with the land than with borders. They are busy with growing their food, and when their crops fail they blame the lack of rain, not the Jews. Also, we live modestly here. They have nothing to envy us for." She turned back to continue putting our dinner together.

When Rozsi came back, she was carrying a newspaper and had a strained expression on her face. "Can I read the newspaper?" I asked, reaching for it. "You would not understand it, it's all political," she said. As Babi opened it, I caught the word "JEWS" in bold black letters. Babi ran her eyes over the page, folded the paper up again, and laid it down on the table. "We'll talk after supper," she said to Rozsi.

The next afternoon, when Babi and Rozsi were out walking in the fields, Molcha and I took the newspaper from the night table where Babi had left it before she went to sleep. We went into the clover field, and while Molcha watched to warn me if anyone came, I tried to read it. The phrases "rounding up" and "slave labor" caught my eye, but most of the words were confusing, and I could not understand all the meanings. Places with strange names— Kamenets-Podolski, Novi Sad—were mentioned.

"Where are these places?" Molcha asked as I tried to pronounce them.

"I don't know," I answered. "Maybe Poland, where Babi said Hitler is."

"Who is Hitler?" Molcha asked.

"Babi says that he is a madman who is turning everybody against the Jews."

"Why?"

"I am trying to find out. It says here that we are bad risks and eat up too much of the bread. We cause bread shortages."

"But we only eat our own bread, so how can we cause a shortage?"

"I don't know."

Molcha ended the discussion. "Let's put the paper back, and you can teach me more Hungarian."

3

Each day we listened to every shred of news the farmers brought back from the Szölös market, hoping that a settlement at the borders would set the trains between Komjaty and Beregszász in motion. Babi's time spent in prayer grew longer. After supper she would put on her angora shawl, take her prayer book, and sit in her armchair facing the front window, becoming so absorbed in her reading that she did not even notice the fading of the light.

One evening, Rozsi and I came in from sitting on the porch to find Babi bent over her book with the bedroom in dark shadows.

"Babi, you always tell me not to ruin my eyes and here you are reading in the dark," said Rozsi, lighting the kerosene lamp.

"I'm not really reading. After you have said these prayers for over fifty years, they become part of you. I just keep the book open in case I forget a word here and there."

"Babi," I asked, "don't you get bored reading the same book all the time?"

"No, Piri, one can never grow bored with this book, because every time I read or recite I find more meaning in the words. It has all the traditions and laws of the Jewish household." Babi closed her book and sat in silence for a while. She always rested like this after her work for the day was finished, and told us that in this way she said thanks for the passing day, asked forgiveness of her sins, and expressed her hope for peace among men.

A week before the eve of Rosh Hashanah, a man hand-delivered a letter from Mother to Babi. Mother had sent it to Aunt Helen in Szölös because mail was still not being delivered in Komjaty. It had taken three weeks for it to reach us.

Father had been called back into the army, but because he was Czech, he had been stripped of his officer's rank, and made a private. My brother-in-law Lajos had been drafted. In Beregszász the people were beginning to feel resentful of the harshness of the newly imposed rules dictated by the Germans.

Mother wrote: "We are in a general upheaval: so many new laws to cope with every day. Our life has changed so much that we don't know what to expect from one day to the next. Mr. Kovacs had to take over the running of our shoe store until Father returns."

Mother was also concerned about us, urging us to get news to her as soon as possible. She asked Rozsi to see about getting me registered in school in case the border remained closed past September.

"I guess Babi's predictions about Hungarian rulers were right," I whispered to Rozsi as soon as Babi left the kitchen.

"She is always right about everything," Rozsi answered me. "We must try to get a letter to Mother as soon as possible so that she knows we are all right. I want to find out if they are coming for Rosh Hashanah.''

Babi came back in. "Just how do you propose to send that letter?"

"Maybe we will find someone going to Szölös who could mail it for us."

Babi narrowed her eyes and bit her upper lip. "How good a friend do you think your Hungarian policeman would be in an emergency?"

Rozsi turned to look directly at Babi. "Friend? I have only spoken to him . . ." She hesitated.

"Do you think he could be trusted to mail the letter right away?"

"I don't know."

Babi looked at me. "You be on the lookout for him, and run in to call Rozsi as soon as you spot him."

"What shall I tell him?" asked Rozsi.

"Tell him the truth. That your mother is worried about us. He should have no trouble understanding that. He knows what is going on." Her tone was harsh.

A few days later, I glimpsed Ferenc at the edge of the woods and ran to tell Rozsi that he was coming. She was on the porch when I got to the house. Too breathless to say anything, I pointed in the direction of the forest. Rozsi immediately went inside and came out with the letter. She walked to the road holding it behind her back, and I followed her. Ferenc reined his horse in at the gate and dismounted. "What a beautiful day," he said. "It is too bad that you can't go for a ride with me."

"No, we can't," said Rozsi. "But we have a big favor to ask you. I wrote a letter to my mother, but have no way of mailing it. Could you mail it for us?" Her voice was shaking, and I was afraid that she might cry.

Ferenc took the letter and put it inside his breast pocket. "Is that all? I am happy to oblige, but it is such a small favor." He brushed Rozsi's shoulder with his hand. "I'll mail it today."

Rozsi's voice relaxed. She looked up at Ferenc. "Thank you."

* * *

Right until the eve of Rosh Hashanah, Babi never gave up hoping for the miracle that would bring the rest of our family to her table. More than once I saw her leave the kitchen and her preparations for the celebratory meal, walk out to the road, face the forest, and search the distance for moving shadows.

"Babi, do you still think they might come?" I questioned when she returned to the kitchen after one of these trips.

"We must never give up. Hope is our salvation."

The big enamel pots were filled to the brim. On the stove the soup simmered, the chicken sizzled, and the tsimmes steamed. Rozsi's fine noodles rested on a large plate, ready to be blended with the golden chicken broth. She polished the brass candlesticks and set the table with as many plates as it would hold. As she worked, I asked, "Rozsi, do you think they will come today?" She motioned me to follow her, and when she was sure Babi could not hear, answered, "If you're smart, you won't get your hopes up."

"Then why are you and Babi pretending?"

"It is not pretending. Babi has prepared this meal for all of us for twenty years. She is following her usual routine."

"But she keeps going out to look for them."

"She has done that for a long time, too. It is part of her ritual."

Not until it was time to light the candles for the New Year's blessing did Babi close the front door. Rozsi and I stood on either side of her as she recited the prayer. She tied the white lace scarf around her head, looked straight up toward the ceiling, and spoke in a hushed voice: "Blessed art thou, O Lord our God, King of the Universe, who has sanctified us by thy commandments and commanded us to kindle the yontif lights."

Babi spent the next day of Rosh Hashanah praying in the synagogue. I sat by her for a little while, but was uncomfortable inside the low building. Both the faces of the women on Babi's side of the room and those of the men on the other side of the room were drawn and pinched.

They chanted in a monotone, crying out occasionally to be judged with mercy. Babi held my hand to unite me with her and the congregation, but I tried to distract myself by looking at the tiny squares of glass inside the windows, at the crooked walls of mortar, and at the sagging mahogany altar that contained the parchment scrolls. Surrounded by this gloom, I could not keep back my tears, and at the first break in the chanting I let go of Babi's hand and slipped out of the room. I spent the rest of the day playing in the temple yard with Molcha.

The next morning, Rozsi came in from milking with a bucket of foamy milk in each hand. "What are you doing up so early?" she asked.

"I was too excited about school to sleep. I heard the roosters crowing, but stayed in bed until you and Babi left the room."

Rozsi put the buckets down on the kitchen bench and spoke to Babi, who was stirring the farina for my breakfast. "Strange," said Rozsi, "this is the first year that I am not going to school, and now Piri is going."

Molcha was waiting for me when I got to her gate. She was nervous about the new language. "I can remember all the words you taught me. You want to hear them?" She recited the simple Hungarian words as if they were parts of a poem.

When we entered the schoolroom, a handsomely dressed young woman stood next to the blackboard in the front. Other children were strolling in. I knew most of them, some older, some younger than I. After the teacher got us seated, she asked us to get up one at a time and recite our names. Each child stood slowly and whispered his or her name. When my turn came I said, "Piri Davidowitz," in a loud, clear voice.

"Now, that is the way I like to hear a name spoken," said the teacher. She spent the rest of the day teaching the Hungarian pronunciation of each of our names, and the Hungarian words for all the things in the classroom. I was the star pupil, and at the end of class she announced that I would be her assistant. I ran home filled with delight to tell Babi and Rozsi the good news. When I found Babi in the field, busy with the last day's harvest, she just commented sarcastically, "Your mother would be overjoyed to hear that you were made a Hungarian translator."

Fall passed, leaving Komjaty looking barren and deserted. People came out of their houses only when they had to. Several times I had come home from school to find Rozsi, wrapped in her shawl, standing on the porch gazing in the direction of the forest. Ferenc had not been by for quite a while.

Babi had found people from time to time who were going to Szölös and would take our letters to be mailed. In November we received a letter from America that was mailed to Aunt Helen in Szölös. Babi ripped it open with nervous fingers. Later, she talked about it with Rozsi.

"They know more about what's going on than we do."

"What do they say?" asked Rozsi.

"The same thing. Sell everything and book passage. How could they understand? To them it is just some land and a house, so you get your price and leave it. No, it is not that easy; you cannot sell your life, and to me this small house, the land, my animals—that is all I know. What do I know about America? I'm an old woman; it is too late for me to run away to a new world. No, I'll just live out my years right here."

That night we got our first snowfall and the roads were covered with uneven drifts. Rozsi walked out on the porch with me as I was leaving for school, and wrapped a scarf around my head so that it covered my mouth. I found Molcha all bundled up, too. In the schoolroom there was a fire in the potbellied stove and our teacher stood by it, warming her fingers.

"You will have to bring firewood starting tomorrow; we have just enough for today. Piri, explain to the children that each of you will have to bring a log starting tomorrow. Otherwise, we'll have to close the school."

When I told Babi and Rozsi what she had asked us to do, Babi looked concerned. "Your teacher does not know these people. They will let her close the school. They care more about their firewood than they do about her school."

Rozsi was surprised. "This never happened before. We always had plenty of wood."

"Changes, changes," said Babi.

We settled in against the snow and wind. The fire in our bedroom was constantly fed with split logs stored behind the stove, which Rozsi and I replenished by trips to the woodpile. We tried to keep a few days ahead so that the wood could dry inside before we used it. Babi was relieved when, in January, school closed down for the rest of the winter; she had been reluctant to let me go out of the house with the snowdrifts almost as high as I was. We left the warmth of our house only to tend to the animals, to bring in water and wood, and to go to the outhouse.

We lived that way until the beginning of March, when school reopened. Then we heard that the trains between Komjaty and Beregszász were running again and that mail delivery was going to resume. I wondered when I would be able to return home.

4

It wasn't until early in April, when Molcha and I were picking violets on the outskirts of the forest, that we saw the mailman coming down the road. We hurried back toward the house to meet him. Rozsi was in the yard hanging wash on the clothesline, and noticing our excitement as we came up to her, she asked, "Did you see Ferenc?"

"No, Rozsi," I said, "it is the mailman; maybe he has a letter from Mother." Turning away to hide her disappointment, Rozsi dropped her clothespins and apron into the laundry basket and walked into the house. With Molcha close behind me, I ran up to the mailman. He handed me the anticipated letter from Mother, and clutching the violets in one hand and the letter in the other, I called goodbye to Molcha on my way back to the house. Babi had come out onto the porch and I gave her the letter and went inside to look for Rozsi. She was in the spare bedroom, staring out of the window that faced the forest. I touched her arm and gave her the violets, and then returned to the porch, where I found Babi on the bench, bent over the letter, tears running down her face.

"Is everyone all right?" I asked anxiously.

Babi folded the letter and put it into her apron pocket. Then she wiped her eyes with the hem of her apron, stood up, and answered, "Everything is fine, Piri. Come, help me catch the biggest chickens in the yard. They are all coming for Passover."

"Who is coming, Babi?"

"Maybe we better take one of the geese, too. There will be so many of us."

"How many?"

"Let's count," said Babi, taking my fingers as though we were going to play a game. She looked down at me and I realized that her small coffee-bean eyes were sparkling for the first time since last fall. Taking my little finger, she counted in a playful, singsong manner. "Your mother, your stepfather, Iboya, and Sandor."

"But Father is in the army."

"Yes, but he is home, he has a leave." I was overjoyed and began to skip around Babi. "Don't you want me to finish counting?" she asked, catching my fingers again. "Lilli, Lajos, and little Manci are also coming. Go call Rozsi, and we'll catch the birds."

In the house, Rozsi was still standing at the window and looked as though she might have been crying.

"Babi sent me to call you. We got a letter from home. They are all coming for Passover."

"Everyone?"

"Yes, Father and Lajos both have leave from the army."

Rozsi's expression brightened; she picked me up under my armpits and swung me around. "When will all this take place?"

"The day after tomorrow. We had better go help Babi catch some chickens and maybe a goose, too."

As we came out onto the porch, Rozsi stopped for a

moment and laughed when she saw Babi luring the chickens. Babi was hunched over, holding an ear of corn in her hand, calling, "Here, pretty; here, pretty." As soon as a hen got close enough to peck at the kernels, Babi snatched it up and, holding the bird up in the air, blew its feathers apart to check the skin for fat. If the skin wasn't yellow enough, she put it down and began all over again.

"Fine helpers you are, letting me do all the picking myself," Babi scolded as she reached into her pocket and gave the letter to Rozsi. "Don't read it now. Help me find two decent birds."

Rozsi looked over the chickens with calculating eyes. "How about that one with the short tail?"

"No, she is one of our best layers. We'll need lots of eggs, too." Finally Babi and Rozsi chose the chickens and Babi tied red rags on their legs.

"Now I am satisfied that we'll have a big pot of chicken soup."

Rozsi nodded her head in answer and started to read Mother's letter as she walked back to the house.

"Can I read it, too?" I asked.

"Come, I'll read it out loud," said Rozsi, sitting down on the porch bench. I sat beside her and listened to her soft voice reading Mother's words. Mother sounded happy because Father had walked in unexpectedly that morning. Lajos, Lilli, and Manci had gone to visit Lajos' parents in Salánk and would come separately.

Babi was in a frenzy all of the next day. While preparing the bedding she explained, "Your mother and father can sleep in the spare bedroom, and you children will sleep on the floor. We'll stuff some straw mattresses. Rozsi can sleep in your bed so that Lilli and Lajos can have Grandpa's bed."

"You mean Rozsi's bed."

"To me it will always be your grandpa's bed."

The next day we kept bumping into each other, as we stopped in the midst of our chores to go out and look for our arriving family. In the late afternoon I spotted them and dashed off the porch. Mother and Father walked together. Father bent over his bicycle, which was loaded down with a large suitcase and several packages. He was wearing an ugly flannel uniform. Mother had changed— her usually smooth skin all puffy. I pulled away from her.

"Didn't you miss me?" she asked, sounding hurt.

"What about me? Will I get a kiss?" Father asked as he bent down to me. I put my arms around his neck and kissed him on the cheek. He still had his bushy sideburns.

Iboya put down the packages she was carrying and hugged me tight. When she let go, I picked up Sandor. He had grown from a baby into a little boy and kept repeating, "This is my sister, Piri, this is Piri," as I held his chunky body in my arms.

Babi and Rozsi came up to us. Rozsi took Sandor from me and kissed him over and over again. Trying to put her short arms around Mother, Babi sobbed, "Why didn't you mention anything in your letters?"

"I didn't want you to worry," Mother answered.

"So how far are you? It looks close." She looked Mother up and down. "And you walked all that distance; I could have sent someone with a wagon, but I didn't know which train you would be on. You just said Friday in your letter."

"We walked slowly," said Father, trying to move us in the direction of the house.

Mother released Babi and put a heavy arm around me. "You have grown prettier. Wait until your friends see you."

"Am I going home with you?"

"Don't you want to?"

"I'm not sure. You said everything changed. Have Ica, Vali, and Milush changed? Will they still like me, even though I am Jewish?"

"You were always Jewish."

"I know, but everything is different."

Mother kissed me and told me not to worry. She looked tired, and when we got to the porch, she sank down on the bench. "I must sit for a while." Rozsi put Sandor down and told Mother she would bring her a cool drink. As Rozsi went into the kitchen, everyone began to speak at once. When Rozsi returned, she handed Mother a large glass of water, which she drank down. Then Mother took off her shoes, and remained sitting on the porch while we took in all the packages.

"What happened to Mother?" I asked Iboya when we got inside.

"She is going to have a baby."

"When?"

"In June. Maybe on your birthday."

Later in the afternoon, Lilli, Lajos, and Manci arrived. Mother called, "Here they come," and we all ran out to meet them. Lilli walked beside Lajos, and Manci clung to her father's back. It seemed so long since I had seen them. Like Sandor, Manci had grown up. When she saw Sandor running toward her, she urged Lajos to put her down. Lajos lowered her to the ground just as Sandor came up and they immediately started chattering. We all stood in the road for a moment watching them.

I was puzzled by Lajos' Hungarian officer's uniform and turned to Iboya to ask, "Why is Lajos wearing that kind of uniform when Father has to wear such an ugly one?"

"I don't know," she answered in a hesitant tone.

"You've grown so, Piri," said Lilli as she put a long arm around me. "Wait until you see the globe Lajos brought for you and Iboya," she added.

Later, in the house, when Lilli hugged Babi, she looked like a mother bending over a child. She was by far the tallest female in our family. "And how is my sweet Babi?" she asked in broken Yiddish. Looking up at her, Babi smiled. "You have forgotten your Yiddish."

"I don't have much chance to speak it and he doesn't help," Lilli replied, pointing toward Lajos.

"Why? I speak Yiddish," Lajos said, carefully pronouncing each word with a heavy Hungarian accent. We all laughed.

"That is the way your father-in-law spoke Yiddish when he married my daughter," said Babi.

"And it was a lucky thing that I learned to speak it well," said Father. "There are several young men in my platoon who have trouble speaking anything but Yiddish."

Pulling his hands out of his trouser pockets, he began to adjust his tie. There was sudden quiet in the large bedroom.

"Well, old man, you carried an officer's responsibilities long enough. Time for the younger men like me to do some work," said Lajos, breaking the silence and coming over to pat Father on the shoulder. "And anyhow, now that things have quieted down, there may just be some pleasant changes."

"When did all this happen to you? No one told me about it," Father questioned as he touched a finger to the first lieutenant's insignia on Lajos' lapel.

"As soon as they found out how good I was," Lajos answered with a salute.

"Come, girls, let's go set the table; it's almost time for seder," said Babi.

After sundown, we were seated around the big mahogany table in the bedroom. Babi and Mother rose, each lighting her own set of candles at either end of the table, their heads covered in lace, their faces glowing in the candlelight.

Looking at them, drawn together by the same ancient tradition, I began to understand the meaning of the expression I had often heard grownups use, "You can graft the branch of a cherry tree onto a peach tree, but it will still bear cherries." Mother had gone a long way from Komjaty, but she was still Babi's daughter. I had seen them together many times before, when a gesture or a nod from one of them rekindled an old memory between them; they could giggle or grow sad together without uttering a word.

After they sat down, Father started the ritual recitation of the Passover story from the Haggadah. He had changed into his regular clothes and was wearing a gray suit with a light blue shirt and dark tie. His blue eyes shone as he called for the four questions traditionally asked by the youngest male child. Sandor, prompted by Mother, asked the questions.

The seder continued and we drank the four glasses of wine at the appropriate places during the reading. The meal ended with tea and the honey cake signifying a sweet year. We sang the traditional songs together, feeling lighthearted as our voices blended in the familiar words. By the time Mother kissed me good night, I had gotten used to her appearance, and my fears about her having changed had vanished.

The next day, while Iboya and I were sitting on the porch, Mother's voice, choked with tears, reached us from the kitchen, "No, I could never do that."

"I loved your brothers and sister, but I sent them with blessings when they wanted to go. What do you think the future holds for these girls, the way things are now?"

"I have thought about it a lot. I can't break up my family. If it were peacetime, maybe I could, I don't know, but with all that is going on right now, I can't send them away. I want them here with me. Whatever comes, we'll face it together. I'm not like you, Mother, I can't be by myself. Not everybody can."

"You were never lonely enough to come back to spend time here with me."

"It's not you, Mama, it's . . . this backward existence. I could never live with it again. I feel alive in the city where people are more civilized. I can talk with them, they understand me."

"Rise, you are fooling yourself. You are living among goyim and you think they are your friends. I just hope you never have to depend on them. They are neighborly, but there is a big difference between neighbors and your own. Only your own can feel your pain."

"They have helped me when I needed them. You were not there when Mayer died; you did not see them look after my little ones for me."

"That kind of crisis is familiar to them: a husband dying, they can understand that. But this is a Jewish problem we are facing. They will not understand."

Iboya and I were shocked by what we were hearing; Babi and Mother were so involved in their discussion that they had forgotten about us on the porch.

"They are talking about sending us away," Iboya said, puzzled.

"They are talking about sending us to America," I answered the question in her voice, as Rozsi and Father turned the corner at the side of the house and came up onto the porch.

"Who is sending you where?" Father asked.

"Babi wants Mother to send us to America."

"You too, Rozsi," said Iboya.

"Nobody is sending you girls anywhere. The war is almost over." Father sat down on the bench beside us. A few moments passed in silence and then Mother came out to call us in for lunch.

After Iboya and I finished up the dishes, Iboya went to her mattress to lie down for a while, and I decided to go call on Molcha. I came to the kitchen threshold and was about to step onto the porch when I overheard Babi speaking in a low and serious tone of voice, her back to me as she faced Father, who was sitting on the bench. Neither of them noticed me standing in the doorway.

"Ignac, I know that you love the girls, and God knows what a wonderful father you have been to them. But you are also a smart man, so I'm going to ask you to let them go to America. They have no future here. Nobody does."

"It isn't as bad as it looks to you, Mama," Father said gently. "The Hungarians have refused to give in to Hitler's demands."

"Ignac, you are an intelligent man. Be realistic. How long can they fight him? No, if they stay . . ." Babi's voice trembled; she turned and saw me on the threshold. "Piri, what are you doing there?"

"I was just going to look for Molcha, Babi."

Babi nodded and walked past me into the main room. She closed the door. I settled myself beside Father on the bench.

"Where did everybody go?" I asked.

"They are walking to the Rika."

"Aren't you going?"

"No, I'm going to take a nap."

"Father, can I ask you something?"

"Yes, of course."

"Why didn't they take away Lajos' officer's uniform? He is Jewish. They took yours away."

"They didn't take mine away because I am Jewish; they

took it away because I was a Czech officer. Lajos was never part of the Czech army; he was drafted into the Hungarian army. The Hungarians don't trust the Czechs, especially in this war. I don't have the uniform, but I still train the new recruits,'' he ended with a forced chuckle.

In the afternoon we had company. A number of the Jewish families came to say hello to Babi's guests. The men asked Father political questions, and they seemed suspicious of Lajos, who was wearing his Hungarian officer's uniform.

I joined Iboya, who was listening to the women talk about the food Babi had prepared and the city clothes that Mother was wearing. Mother became very talkative and gay, making them all laugh. Then she turned to me and suggested I bring out the globe Lajos had given to Iboya and me.

I went into the spare room, and brought the globe back to a corner of the porch. The teen-agers all gathered around and took turns rotating it. At one point the men came over to trace out the border questions they had been discussing. Hitler and Germany were mentioned many times before they all left.

That night at our second seder, Lajos became solemn and fidgety. ''Don't you feel well?'' Babi asked.

''He is just upset at the way the guests felt about his Hungarian uniform,'' Lilli tried to explain in her best Yiddish.

After dinner we decided to go to bed early so that everyone would be rested for the day of travel ahead. Mother came over to us on our straw mattresses, and as she bent to kiss me, I asked, ''Anyuka, am I going home with you tomorrow?'' But I already knew the answer. I had heard her tell Rozsi that she would need her help with the new baby because Lilli was going to spend the rest of Lajos' leave at his base in Prague. When Rozsi objected to leaving Babi at the beginning of the spring planting season, Mother said that I would stay on to finish my school year in Komjaty. Rozsi protested that I could not do her chores, but Mother reminded her that I was now just two years younger than Rozsi herself had been when she first came to Komjaty.

"No, I need Rozsi at home," Mother said to me. "You must stay here to take care of Babi and finish school. You will come home when Rozsi comes back."

I accepted Mother's statement although I was feeling very confused. Part of me wanted to go home, but another part liked the thought of taking Rozsi's place with Babi, and still another part did not want Rozsi to leave, either.

When I woke up in the late morning, everyone was packed and ready to go. A neighbor came with his wagon to take them to the train station, but Mother refused to get into it. "I would rather walk than ride on this bumpy road." Father put his bike up into the wagon and said that he would walk with Mother. Babi asked if I wanted to go with them part of the way.

"No," I said firmly, surprised by my own decision.

"All right," said Babi. "We'll stay."

They all took turns kissing me goodbye.

"School will be over before you know it," said Mother, "and then a few weeks after that you'll come home."

Father picked me up and whispered in my ear, "Don't forget, you are still my little girl."

Iboya was the last one to say goodbye to me. She left me the globe and promised to write. Watching the wagon go down the road with Mother and Father walking behind, my eyes clouded with tears. I ran back into the empty house, closed the bedroom door behind me, fell onto my bed, and started to sob.

A long time later, Babi knocked on the door instead of just walking in. "Come, Piri," I heard her say, "let's have something to eat." It was already past noon, and I realized that I had not eaten any breakfast.

"That is how it is after the house is full of people and then they all have to leave," she said as I ate the matzo brei she had made for me.

5

A week later, I twisted my ankle while Molcha and I were climbing the rocks on the bank of the Rika. I did not go to school the next day, but took my schoolbooks out onto the porch after Babi left for the fields, propped my leg up on a chair, and was busy writing my lessons when Ferenc stopped at our gate. He tied his horse and came up to join me on the porch. After examining my swollen ankle, he asked how it happened. I answered that I had twisted it and told him that I was alone. "Babi is in the field, and Rozsi is in Beregszász. My mother is going to have a baby, and Rozsi has to stay with her."

He sat down next to me and asked, "How is your grandmother feeling these days?"

"She has been very tired," I began. "I don't think she sleeps much during the nights, I can hear her twisting and turning in her bed."

"What do you think has been bothering her?" Ferenc asked.

I hesitated before telling him, but I wanted to hear what he would say. "I think she has been trying to talk my mother into sending me and my sisters to America."

"That would be a smart thing to do, and she shouldn't go on living here alone, either," he said. "She should sell her property, move to Beregszász, and live with your mother. She'd be closer to things there. She's too isolated here, and it isn't safe. Please tell her what I said. Now I'd better move on before she finds me here."

I did not want Ferenc to leave. "Don't go yet. She doesn't mind when you talk to me. It's only when it's Rozsi that she gets upset."

He laughed and got up. "When is Rozsika coming back?"

"After Mother has the baby. It's expected in a few weeks. It might even be born on my birthday."

"When is that?"

"June 10th."

"Then I may not see her. I'm being transferred," he said. "Please explain to Rozsi about my new orders. And I hope you have a nice birthday." He left the porch and watered his horse. Then he waved to me, sadness lingering in his face, as he rode off.

Soon after Ferenc left, Babi came from the fields with a special treat of wild strawberries laced on a long grass stem. While we were eating supper, she said, "You had a visitor," and I knew from the tone of her voice that she meant Ferenc.

"Oh, you saw the horseshoe prints around the trough."

"Yes, and I also saw the horse and his rider and so did everyone else in the fields. You don't think such a sight can go by unnoticed."

She sounded amused, and I was surprised. "You're not angry."

"What good would it do me if I were?"

Later that evening, Babi asked me, "What did you and Ferenc talk about?"

I knew I had to be careful about how much I said. "First he asked how you are."

"How I am! How Rozsi is would be more to the truth."

"No, Babi, you just don't like him, but he really did ask about you. He even asked me to give you a message."

"This I would like to hear."

"I told him about your wanting to send us to America."

"You told him that?"

"Yes, Babi."

"Piri, you can't go repeating to strangers things that are said in our house."

I was silent. I had said too much again. But Babi asked me, "What did he think I should do?" When I didn't answer, she repeated the question.

"He said that you should sell and move to Beregszász so you can be closer to things."

"What things?"

"He didn't say. He just said it was not safe for you here, so isolated from everything."

"Suddenly everybody is telling me what to do. I managed all right up to now. I'll just have to take my chances. Did he ask you when Rozsi is coming back?"

I did not answer immediately, so she added, "Or did you just tell him?"

"I don't remember," I said.

"Did he say when he would be back?"

"He is being transferred. He won't be coming this way any more." I resented the expression on Babi's face as she looked up from her sewing.

School was over at the end of May, and by the time my birthday came around, I was spending most of my days roaming the fields with Molcha.

Joli was born June 16. Rozsi sent a letter telling us that Mother and the baby girl were fine. Lajos' leave was over and Lilli and Manci were expected back from Prague any day.

Babi was happy to hear that it was all over. I realized from her expression of relief how concerned she had been. "Well, you know that your mother should stop having children, she is not so young any more."

"How old is Mother?" I asked.

"She will be thirty-nine on her next birthday."

I started to think about what it would be like to take care of and play with a little sister, and began to get excited about going to see her. But when Rozsi returned to Komjaty toward the end of July, I became uncertain again. Whenever Rozsi spoke to Babi about life in Beregszász, I listened very carefully for news of any changes. Babi asked many questions, and they spoke about political changes, but their main topic was the well-being of the family.

When I told Rozsi about Ferenc's visit, she listened with anticipation, her face flushed, anxious to hear every word. I felt bad having to tell what he said. Stalling, I first told her about the message for Babi.

"Did he have a message for me?"

"He was sorry that you were not here."

"Did he say when he would be coming again?"

"Rozsi, Ferenc is not going to come. He has been

transferred." She stood up abruptly and said, "It is for the best. I would not want another confrontation with Babi. And what is the use of it, anyway?"

A heavy feeling had been pressing in my chest at the thought of leaving Komjaty. I would miss Babi, Rozsi, and Molcha, just as I missed Mother, Iboya, and my friends when I first came to Komjaty. But now I wasn't so sure about Beregszász and the people there. I felt confused and decided to talk to Rozsi about it.

"As usual," she said, "you have been listening to too many stories. A few days after you get home you'll be in school and so busy that you'll forget about all these things."

"No, I'll miss Komjaty a lot. You and Babi especially."

"So next summer you'll come back."

"What if by next summer . . ." I paused and then said, "Or perhaps Mother will decide to send us to America."

The Sunday of my departure arrived before I had fully faced the fact of leaving Komjaty. Babi and Rozsi had filled baskets with dried mushrooms, prunes, lekvár, and jams. My clothes were packed in one large suitcase.

"Eat your breakfast," Babi urged as she watched me dawdling over the piece of egg on my fork. "You will have to carry two heavy baskets." My head ached, and my stomach was all mixed up.

"I'll just drink the milk, Babi."

Shaking her head from side to side, Babi offered a compromise. "You have to eat one egg, too." I washed down the buttery egg with milk and picked up the box I had prepared to leave with Molcha.

"Go, she is waiting in the road," said Babi, opening the oak door to the porch. As soon as Molcha saw the door open, she ran up onto the porch. Babi closed the door and left us alone.

"So," Molcha said, "I guess you will be leaving on the train."

"Maybe you can come to visit me in Beregszász sometime. Maybe next summer if I don't come here."

"Why wouldn't you come here next summer?"

"I don't know." I handed her the box containing paper,

a pen, ink, and a blotter. "I'm leaving these things for you so you'll be able to write to me and tell me everything that's happening."

"Like what?" she questioned as she took the box.

Rozsi opened the door. "We have to get started. Walking will be slow because we have so much to carry."

Molcha and I hugged, practically crushing the box between us. "*Szervusz*, Piri, thank you for the things," said Molcha. She rescued the box, turned quickly, and ran off the porch. When she stopped to wave, I saw that she was crying.

"*Szervusz*, Molcha," I called. "I'll write first."

I turned toward the house, hoping Rozsi would not see the tears in my eyes. Babi stood on the threshold of the kitchen, her arms open to embrace me.

"It's all right, little lamb, some things are hard for all of us. That is the way it goes with life." She wiped away my tears with the hem of her apron. "Here, I have something to take away the sadness of parting." She reached into her apron pocket and brought out a small box, opened it, and lifted out the garnet earrings she had given me for my birthday.

"You forgot about these, didn't you? Well, I want you to take them home with you and wear them on special occasions so that you'll remember your Babi." Her worn brown fingers shook as she hooked them through my earlobes. When she had finished, she smoothed my face first with tender fingers, then with her own face, which she rubbed against mine. I tried to say goodbye, but the words would not come out. I kissed her wrinkled face, hoping that she would understand. Rozsi picked up the large suitcase and one of the baskets. I picked up the remaining two, thankful for the excuse to turn away from Babi and start moving.

"I'll come back right after I've put Piri on the train, most likely in time for lunch, if the train is not late," Rozsi said. Babi walked down to the road with us. "Godspeed," she called after us.

Fifteen minutes later we stopped to rest and I turned to look back at Komjaty. Babi's house seemed so small in the distance. I wondered if she were still standing in the road, trying to see us.

"Babi isn't in the road," I said to Rozsi.

"No, she went back in just after we left. Come on, let's move. We'll stop again soon," Rozsi urged as she looked toward the forest. The leaves on the maples and oaks skirting the road had just begun to turn their autumn bronze, yellow, and red, and the forest evergreens contrasted harshly with the bright colors. In the distance I could hear the rushing waters of the Rika. Soon we were closed into a separate world by the walls of the forest and the sound of the water; no sight or sound from the outside penetrated this world.

We rested on the bank of the river. I looked down into the water, watching the swiftly flowing current. We could not hear each other above the noise, but Rozsi took a pendant watch out of the bosom of her dress, checked the time, and motioned that we should start walking. I was grateful to move on. My thoughts drifted back to that early spring day when I had seen the uniformed bodies floating in the water. With Father and Lajos in the army, my imagination was creating awful pictures. Why did I think of such terrible things, I wondered.

Coming out into the open clearing with the bright sun and blue sky to greet us lightened my mood. The Komlos station was in sight. "We made good time," said Rozsi, checking her watch, "It's only ten o'clock."

The big coal-burning train came screeching down the tracks with large clouds of black smoke puffing from its smokestack. The wheels stopped abruptly, and we picked up the baggage and climbed aboard. After I was settled, Rozsi went to talk to the conductor about looking after me and helping me off the train in Beregszász. Then she hugged and kissed me goodbye and gave me instructions. "Take care of yourself," she called over her shoulder as she left the train.

The whistle blew and the wheels began to turn. I leaned out of the window to wave goodbye to Rozsi and Komjaty.

BEREGSZÁSZ

6

It was exciting to be back in Beregszász; the big houses and city people generated a kind of energy that was absent in Komjaty. My whole family turned out to welcome me at the train station. Mother, Lilli, and Iboya carried off the suitcase and baskets. I ran over to Manci and Sandor, who were standing near the baby buggy.

"She is big, not the way I pictured her," I said. Joli cooed and waved her arms. With her sparkling blue eyes and square shoulders, she resembled Sandor and my father; the three of them made their own group in the family.

When we got to Gyár Street, I was grateful to find it deserted as I was not ready to face my friends. Mother closed our gate and walked us into the kitchen. Iboya and Lilli took the children into our bedroom.

"You must be hungry," Mother said, as she removed the stove ring under the red enamel pot, exposing it to the coals. A few minutes later she dipped a spoon into the simmering mixture and filled a plate with hot pörkölt. The sight of large chunks of veal held together by a thick paprika gravy made my mouth water. "Eat first," she urged. "Then you can wash, change your clothes, and go out to see your friends." I savored the tender and spicy pörkölt, so different from Babi's bland dishes. As I finished, Lilli, holding the baby, appeared in the doorway.

"Mother wants to transform you back into a city girl," she said, as she handed Joli over to her. Cradling the baby in her left arm, Mother sat down in the armchair beside the kitchen table, and with her right hand, opened her blouse. Joli turned her attention to the breast and Mother caught my eyes watching intently. "She sucks the way you eat," she said jokingly, "anxious for every drop. Come to think of it, you nursed the same way."

Mother watched as Joli grew drowsy in her arms. After a few more minutes, she rose with the baby and walked toward her bedroom to put Joli down in the crib. When she returned to the kitchen, she filled the tub with water from large pots that had been warming on the stove, and I sat down in it. Holding a bar of soap in her left hand and the brush in the other, Mother proceeded to rub and scrub, determined to get me clean and shining. She even tried to wash the dark bruises off my bony legs.

"They are from the heavy water buckets hitting up against me as I carried them from Tercsa's well," I explained.

"And climbing and falling," added Mother.

"I am going to miss Komjaty," I reflected.

"I think I got you home just in time or you would have turned into another Rozsi." Mother studied my face. "What does Rozsi do all day while my mother is out in the fields?"

"She looks after the chickens, geese, and ducks; she gathers eggs, milks the cows, gives them water, works in the vegetable garden, cooks, and takes Babi her lunch if she doesn't come home for it. She cleans the house and sings," I finished.

"Sings? Doesn't she talk to anybody all day?"

"There is nobody around during the day."

"What about the girls across the road—Molcha's sisters?"

"They are busy during the day helping their mother around the house. Rozsi talks to Babi in the evening when they sit and sew."

"But she needs to be with people her own age," Mother commented, as she gave my elbow a hard scrub.

"She visits with neighbor girls on the Sabbath. They all get together then."

Mother and Lilli exchanged glances. I stood up in the tub, and Lilli poured clean rinse water over my sudsy body. At that point, the two little ones came into the kitchen, their hands covered with wet sand. They giggled at seeing me undressed. Manci looked into the tub and rinsed her hands, Sandor copied her; they giggled again and ran out of the kitchen.

I bent over and Mother poured warm water on my head. Cupping the soap in the palm of her hand, she began to vigorously lather my scalp and hair. After two such soapings and several clear rinses, Lilli brought over the final vinegar rinse, which Mother slowly drained through my matted hair.

"There, your hair finally squeaks and shines again, the way it should," Mother said, wrapping it up in a towel. I put on the dress Lilli had picked out for me, and went to sit in the yard. Mother fine-combed my long hair and clipped off the straggly ends. Then, after a final survey, she opened the big gate.

I walked to the gate and looked out, running my eyes up and down each side of the street. The cement sidewalks seemed so clean and white in the glare of the sun.

"Nobody is out there."

"Milush and Vali probably walked to the park to play in the shade. Why don't you and Iboya go and join them," Mother offered.

I shook my head. I did not want to see my friends yet, and I walked inside, into the children's room, where Lilli was putting my clothes away.

"Have you and Manci come to live with us?" I asked.

"No, I still have the apartment, but we do sleep over occasionally. Why, what's the matter?"

"I was just wondering. I was away for a long time," I said, not wanting her to see my fear of things having changed while I was away.

Late in the afternoon, while Iboya and I were sitting on the porch, Milush and Vali came through the gate. They were in their bathing suits, on the way back from the strand. They walked toward us hesitantly.

"*Szervusz, szervusz,* we came to see if you were home," they greeted me.

We were all talking busily when Mother came out with a pitcher of raspberry punch. "Isn't your mother coming over?" she asked Vali.

"I'll go and get her," said Vali, running off. Soon Mrs. Veligan appeared, with Vali alongside her.

"You should have come along, Mrs. Davidowitz, it was not at all crowded," Mrs. Veligan said as she stepped onto the porch. "You could do with a little sun. Look how nice your girls look with their brown faces. My God, Piri! You look so tall. Stand up so I can see you." She pushed Vali and me into a back-to-back position. "See, she has grown half a head. It is that country air, and I bet your grandmother fed you lots of milk and eggs. Nothing like that for growing children. You can't get much of that here any more. Getting more scarce all the time."

Lilli, closing her book, came to join us, with Manci and Sandor trailing behind her. Mother poured the punch into glasses and handed them around. As we stood there, I felt relieved, relaxing for the first time in that whole long day. I was home in Beregszász.

7

When school began in September, life resumed its routine for Iboya and me. Politics seemed remote from us all as we were kept busy with our studies in school and with our chores and projects at home. Lilli was still at our house most of the time; she and Mother read and wrote their postcards together. I never had to ask whether or not they had received mail from Father or Lajos; their voices and expressions told me as soon as I came into the house. Rozsi wrote to us often to keep Mother from worrying about her and Babi. Frequent letters from Molcha told me about her progress in school and the local gossip.

Winter arrived just before Christmas vacation, and snow covered the streets of Beregszász. We had to use both coal and wood in our classroom stove in order to melt the frost on the large windowpanes. During the holidays, not having school to absorb my thoughts, I became more aware of

Father's absence. Hanukkah did not seem the same without him.

Mother stayed in a bad mood for days, did not say silly things to make us laugh or sing, but only spoke to us when she had something to tell us. We stopped turning on the radio because they had suspended newscasts, playing only sermons and Christmas carols. Mother tried to go through the rituals of Hanukkah and lit the candles the first few nights, giving us the customary treats. But, without Father, we could not sing the traditional songs and we gave up lighting the candles and playing dreidel games before the holiday was over.

Milush and Vali came by early on Christmas Eve and entered our kitchen flushed with excitement over their holiday. "We came to call for you. The carolers are down the street."

Iboya and I looked toward Mother, but she shook her head no.

"We can't go this year," Iboya started to explain as Milush and Vali looked at each other. "It is because our father is away . . ." They did not wait for Iboya to finish but turned around and left without saying another word. I waited, hoping that the carolers would stop in as they had in years before and ask, "May we praise Jesus?" Mother had let them sing and then gave them small pastries to eat. But they did not stop at our house, and remembering those other Christmases and how much a part of the festivities we had been, I felt sad.

I began to pay more attention to Joli as the winter went on and the children played in the kitchen. She grew bigger, more animated, more curious about Sandor and Manci as she watched them. In my arms, she smelled of soap, baby powder, and mother's milk and felt like white velvet. In these moments I recalled the scornful expression on Babi's face as she said, "A new baby in these times! Tsu! Tsu!" When I told Mother that Babi did not think that having a baby in wartime was a good idea, Mother grew thoughtful before she answered, "God works in strange ways. I think Joli was just what we needed!"

"Mother," I continued, "do you believe in the same God that Babi does?"

"There is only one God. Your grandmother just believes more than most of us."

"Do you believe that if you tear something on the Sabbath, God will strike you? I tried it out, and He didn't do anything."

Mother tried to pretend that she was angry, but I could see the smile in her green eyes. "You tested God? I'm beginning to understand Babi's concern about you. What else have you done to test God?"

Seeing that she wasn't very upset, I told her that once, in Komjaty, while the Sabbath candles were being lit, I stood outside, picked some grapes, ate them, and waited to see what would happen to me, thinking that perhaps the whole trellis would fall down and kill me instantly. Instead, Rozsi had come out to get me and asked why I had jumped when she came up behind me. When I told her what I'd done, she explained that God was too busy to be bothered by every little thing I did, but that didn't mean He didn't see every little thing. And, she added, if the trellis had fallen, she and Babi would have been hurt and they were innocent.

"Did you ever let my mother know this?"

"No, just Rozsi."

Lilli opened the kitchen door just then, letting in a strong gust of wind. She had a newspaper tucked under her arm, and I thought she had probably also bought some cigarettes in the tobacco shop. I had seen her smoking a few times while she walked outside the house and I wondered if Mother knew. Lilli took off her coat and shook the snow from it before hanging it on the hook.

"You want me to read you the front page while you stir the soup?" she asked Mother.

"No, I'll look at it later," said Mother. "Why don't you set the table, Piri, while Lilli washes the children's hands. And call Iboya from the other room." I knew that all discussions for that evening were ended.

*   *   *

One day, instead of coming straight home from school, Iboya and I stopped in at Farkas & Földes to get some notebooks and look through the new rental books. It was already dusk by the time we got to Tinodi Street. From the street lights high up on their poles, yellow beams lit our way. The snow crunched under our boots as we walked, and becoming aware of the time, we walked faster, fearing Mother's anger at our being out so late. We had reached the little synagogue on the other side of Tinodi Street when we heard loud shouting and saw several old men, prayer shawls still over their shoulders, running from the court-yard into the street. Three boys were among the men with sticks in their hands.

"Stop," I screamed, "or I'll get the police."

Seeing us directly across the street from the synagogue, they yelled, "There are two of those Jew girls," and then came toward us. We started to run as fast as we could. Our schoolbags smacked against our backs, and we could hear the boys gaining on us.

"Dumb Jew bitches, we'll pound your asses, you won't get away. Get the one with the pigtails, the one who yelled she would call the police." They mimicked my voice. "What police is she going to tell? As if they cared about our beating up some old Jews."

Just then two men stepped out of the shadows at the corner. "Hey," called one of the men to the boys, "aren't you ashamed of yourselves, chasing after two little girls?" They walked into the street, putting themselves between us and the three boys, but Iboya and I kept running, not even looking back to see how they stopped the boys. We did not turn around until we reached our front gate—four blocks from Tinodi Street—and by then we could not see them. Bolting the gate after us, we ran into the kitchen.

Mother was sitting in the armchair nursing Joli while sounds of music came from the salon. As we slammed the door behind us, she looked up with a start and put her breast back inside her blouse. Her eyes asked the question "What happened?" even before she spoke.

While Iboya and I leaned against the kitchen door pant-ing, Mother went to the bedroom and put Joli down in the crib. Then, buttoning her blouse as she walked back toward us, she asked, "Why are you so out of breath?"

Iboya spoke first. "There were three boys, they came out of the synagogue on Tinodi Street and chased us with sticks until two men stepped out from the corner courtyard where the Markowitzes live and came between us. One of them yelled at the boys."

"Then what happened?" Mother interrupted.

"We don't know. Iboya and I just kept running until we got here," I answered.

"Why were they? Why were they running out of the synagogue holding sticks?"

"I don't know if they came from inside the synagogue; we just saw them running from the courtyard. I also heard glass breaking, maybe it was the windows. It was dark already and we were across the street. I think I recognized one of them—Imre Kurti." Iboya stopped talking and slowly sat down on one of the kitchen chairs.

"Shut off the radio," Mother called harshly into the salon. Lilli obeyed instantly and ran into the kitchen. She looked us up and down, then came over and slid my schoolbag off my shoulder.

"Are you all right?" she asked softly. Mother came close to Lilli and whispered, "Vandalism at the synagogue. God only knows what must have happened. You are sleeping here tonight. I am not letting you and Manci walk home alone." Lilli's face, as she listened, became as red as Mother's.

"Let's get their coats off," Lilli said, looking at me. I could feel the cold stickiness on my neck and in my armpits, and Iboya and I were still breathing heavily.

Sandor and Manci, sitting on their small bench, watched us and asked questions, but no one knew what to tell them. Joli began to cry and Lilli went to pick her up. She came back with Joli in her arms and sat down on the other little bench opposite Sandor and Manci, her long legs stretched out in front of her. She set Joli down on top of the picnic table and talked to her: "Joli doesn't like to be alone in the bedroom. She wants to be here with Sandor and Manci. No fun for Joli alone, isn't that so, baby?"

"She is probably hungry. I didn't finish feeding her. Now with all of this confusion, I don't think I should give her any more," Mother said.

"Can she stay and eat with us, can she?" asked Sandor.

"Oh yes, she likes to eat grown-up food, better than milk," continued Lilli.

Mother managed to put dinner on the table, and we all ate, but her face remained flushed during our meal. Later that evening, while she and Lilli did the dishes and Iboya and I were in our bedroom washing up, I heard Mother as she spoke to Lilli in a hushed tone: "My mother was right, I should have tried to send the girls to America. Maybe it's not too late. I will have to go and find out if there still is a chance. I don't know what to do about Etu. According to her last letter, she has no intention of quitting school and coming home from Budapest as I asked her to. I don't understand why all my daughters are so strong-willed." Lilli answered her in a voice too low for me to hear, and after that I heard only the sounds of dishes being put away. Iboya and I slept close to each other that night.

8

A few days later we returned home from school to find Lilli alone in the kitchen. "Where's Mother?" we asked in unison as the door opened and Mother came in. She was dressed in her best clothes. Taking off her coat and handing it to Iboya, she sat down heavily on one of the kitchen chairs and began to speak. "I ran my feet off, going to all the places where people told me I could get visas to send you girls to America. People don't know what they are talking about. You can't get passage on a boat no matter what. There are all the Americans going home with their families. Then there are all the people who already have their visas and who have already applied. All I can tell you children is that I tried everything. I pleaded, I cried, I tried to bribe. Nothing made an impression. They hardly even listened. I guess they've heard it all before. You should have seen all the people waiting in lines to speak to the officials. Women with babies in their arms. Everybody with a story to tell and nobody to listen. One clerk told me, 'Listen, lady, if I had any influence I would get myself on a boat to America. You think I like what's going on?' "

Mother bent down and picked up her purse. She took out a bulging envelope, and as she held it up I could see that it was filled with bank notes that Babi had sent Mother for our passage. "I'll have to try to get this back to my mother. Maybe she can buy back a piece of the land she sold. She's owned that land for as long as I can remember. It's not the rain that's made those fields fruitful, it's her endless, untiring love. She'll never understand that her land could not buy passage to America for her grand-daughters."

We all stood quietly, waiting for her to finish, hoping that she would feel better after she had told us everything. It was not like Mother to be so upset. She usually did not let disappointments bother her. "You bounce back like yeast dough," Father used to tease her. "No punch can keep you down." But Mother was down now. She sat in the chair and stared past us until Joli started to whimper. Then, with a start, she pulled herself up. "Who knows, maybe it is for the best after all? What would this house be like without my daughters?"

The spring of 1941 also brought some changes to our school routine. Instead of play during recess, we now had drills and group gymnastics like soldiers. We had to buy navy shorts and white shirts; they gave us large wooden hoops and batons, and we were taught to do tricks with them. We learned to do push-ups, to jump through the hoops, and to use the batons as swords in fencing exercises.

Ica Molnar and I were put into the same group and started walking back and forth to school together. But we did not confide our secrets to each other as we had before I went to Komjaty. Ica's parents and mine had been good friends, frequently going into each other's back yards to converse together. But since my return I had only seen our mothers exchange greetings on the street. Ica and I could sense the new limits to our relationship.

Just before Passover, Mother and Lilli received the first cards from the men in almost two months. Father's card seemed to jolt Mother out of a depression, and she cried as she read it over and over.

"When was that card sent?" Lilli asked.

"Almost three weeks ago."

"Lajos' card is almost four," Lilli exclaimed. She and Mother beamed at each other in spite of their tears and exchanged postcards.

The first week in June we received a surprise visit from a woman about Mother's age accompanied by a girl my age and a boy of seven. She introduced herself as Mrs. Gerber. "My husband wrote to me that he is in your husband's battalion," she said as Mother walked with her toward the salon.

"He asked that I come and meet you so that if one of us gets mail and the other doesn't, we can check with each other and be in touch," she said after she had seated herself on the chair in the salon. Mother introduced us to Mrs. Gerber, and she, in turn, introduced us to Judi and Pali. The women talked for a while, giving each other all the information they had received in the past months from their husbands. Then Mother went into the kitchen and brought back holiday cakes and tea. She was playing hostess again, a role that she loved, and she talked about Father without stopping. Mrs. Gerber invited us to visit her the next Saturday. "I have a cherry tree full of cherries, and they should be ripe by then."

We all decided to call on the Gerbers the following Saturday. Judi Gerber and I climbed up into the tree with a basket and picked the ripe fruit for everybody.

"You realize that we are picking cherries on the Sabbath and nobody seems to notice," I said.

"We are not religious," Judi answered. "We don't bother with tradition and holidays, we are only Jewish by birth."

Beginning with that Sabbath, Judi and I became friends.

We waved and talked to each other on the playground. She didn't have many friends because the other girls said she was odd and standoffish, but she really wasn't once you got to know her.

"Funny we never talked before," I said to her one day. "You were always with your friends."

"I'm not so friendly with them any more. I feel closer to you now."

Judi had come from Budapest when her father's company transferred him to Beregszász before the army drafted him. She lent me some of her books from the school in Budapest and told me that the school had been a progressive one where the students discussed all kinds of ideas and where there were no rigid routines.

I told Iboya some of the things Judi had said. "Don't pick up too many of her ideas," Iboya answered, "or you will become as unpopular as she."

Mother and Mrs. Gerber continued to see each other, and they often talked about Budapest. "My daughter Etu is there in the Gymnasium," Mother said to Mrs. Gerber one afternoon when we were all sitting in our back yard. "I have asked her to come home, but she wants to finish the year."

"Don't ask her to come back here," Mrs. Gerber replied. "She would be much better off there in an emergency. There is less conflict in the big cities because people are not that easily influenced by propaganda. What can she do here? I wish I were back there. We went to the opera and the theater and had marvelous friends."

"Yes," said Mother. "I lived there for a while when I was a young woman; I stayed with one of my sisters who is now in America. How I loved the theater! That was what I missed most of all when I came here. What a long time ago all of that was!"

"But she still remembers all of the plays she saw," said Lilli. "My mother would have made a good actress. You should see her play out some of the parts."

Mother and Mrs. Gerber's conversation turned to food rationing, and Lilli excused herself to take a walk to the tobacco store. She returned with a newspaper, holding up the front page for Mother and Mrs. Gerber to read. The headlines were twice the usual size: HUNGARY JOINS GERMANY TO INVADE RUSSIA. Judi and I left the shade of the chestnut tree and read over our mothers' shoulders.

"Lucky for us that Mr. Kovacs is past forty," Mother said. "He will be able to continue to run the store for us. Without him, we'd lose our weekly income."

"With this general draft in effect, there won't be many men left," commented Mrs. Gerber. "Hitler has come to claim his payment for helping the Hungarians take back Ruthenia and the Czechoslovak and Ukrainian lands. He's going to leave Hungary a country of old men, women, and children."

9

In September I entered the fifth grade. Gymnastics were extended to two hours a day. "Soon you won't have time to learn," Mother commented when I told her about it.

"They are training them for the army," said Lilli.

"Bite your tongue," was Mother's quick reply.

Iboya joined a subdivision of the Red Cross in charge of individual street detail. They enforced blackout drills by inspecting all of the windows, and they were also trained in first aid.

Toward the end of the month a postcard came from Father saying that his company was being transferred and would pass through Beregszász on or about October 6. Mrs. Gerber appeared with a similar postcard from her husband. She and Mother pooled their rations over the next few days and bought as much flour, sugar, eggs, and butter as they could. They made us pick the walnut tree clean. We peeled the outside green covering off the nuts until our hands were stained jet black. Mrs. Gerber and Mother sat on the porch, cracking the hard shells and chopping up the walnut meats, which were still moist with milk. There was no time to let them dry out.

Lilli's hands became busier than I had ever recalled seeing them. She rolled and filled strudels with nuts and sugar and grated lemon peel from morning until dark. Mother piled the split logs into the bread oven, lit them, and after they had burned down, filled the oven with all the pastries they had prepared.

At dawn on the morning of October 6, our two families went to the main railroad station at the other end of Beregszász, to sit on the benches with our bundles and wait for the train that would pass by with Father and his men. Jumping up every time a train moved over the tracks, Mother talked to all the conductors and attendants, hoping to get some information. They had none. When it grew dark, Lilli, Iboya, Judi, and I took the children and went back to our houses while Mother and Mrs. Gerber continued their vigil, taking naps in turn and watching the bundles. We returned to the station in the morning with breakfast for them. They looked tired but refused to go home to freshen up while we remained at the station. We went through the same routine for three more days until, disheartened, Mother and Mrs. Gerber were finally persuaded by the train officials to return to their homes.

That night after we had all fallen asleep, Mother was awakened by a knock on her window. By the time she had wrapped her robe around her and looked out the window, Father was knocking on the guest bedroom door at the back of the house, waking Lilli and Manci. Soon we were all crowded around him. Mother picked Joli up so she could meet her father for the first time. In spite of the hour and the confusion, Joli seemed to understand that this was her moment. Mother handed her to Father, and she snuggled into his arms and stroked his prickly face. Wanting to be held too, Sandor began to call, "Daddy, Daddy," to get Father's attention. Still holding Joli, Father sat down on the divan next to a sleepy and confused Manci, who sat and chewed on her nightgown in silence while Sandor climbed onto his lap. Iboya and I approached the divan shyly, waiting our turn to be held.

Mother was wide awake and filled with concern. "You

ran away? What can happen to you? You must be hungry. Where are they taking you? How is Mr. Gerber?"

Father smiled and answered her last question. "I left Mr. Gerber in charge. Rise, don't worry. We are not sure where we are going, but it could be the Russian front. Do you have my brother Srul's address just in case?"

"Yes, I do. Ignac, take care. I want you home again."

"How are you and the children getting along?"

"No problems. Mr.Kovacs is being generous, he gives us enough to live on."

"Are you getting my army pay checks?"

I could see the sudden question on Mother's face, but she quickly smiled and answered, "Yes, no problem, we are managing very well."

"It won't be for much longer," Father said. "The Russians are very strong. And even if we are captured by the Russians, I am sure that would be better for us than Hitler's succeeding."

As he spoke to Mother, he kissed us each in turn and got up. He embraced Mother, pulling her close. For once she did not pull away from him and scold, "Ignac, the children!" She remained very still for a few seconds and then drew away. "You must not stay longer."

Lilli stepped down from the threshold and flew into his arms with a cry, "Oh, Ignac." As she looked up at him unashamed of her flowing tears, I realized that Lilli loved Father in a different, grown-up way—not Mother's way, but not our way either. They were like very close friends.

"Do you think Lajos will be going, too?" she asked as she separated from him.

"No, Lilli, I think they have forgotten that he is a Jew. Hold fast and we'll soon be home. Look after your mother."

Mother was standing with the bundles. Father shook the contents of his backpack out on the divan—a few slices of dry zwieback—and refilled it with the strudel. "Now I must run."

We all went with him to the gate and watched as he and

Mother embraced. Then Father was gone. Slowly Mother turned back from the gate. Her cheeks were wet with tears, but she spoke to us firmly, telling us all to go back to bed. She picked up Joli, who was still repeating, "Daddy, Daddy," and carried her off, not turning around toward us again. Startled by her abruptness, we all went back to bed.

10

As I was walking home alone from school one day late in October, a woman with an infant in her arms approached me and asked in a wavering voice, "Do you speak Yiddish?"

I nodded.

"I'm running away from Slovakia, and we are hungry. Can you point me to a Jewish door?"

"Follow me, I'm on my way home. I'm sure my mother will give you something to eat," I said in Yiddish.

The woman followed me, walking close to the houses. When we reached our kitchen, I started to explain to Mother, but she pushed me aside and lifted the infant out of the black peasant shawl around the woman's shoulders.

"The child needs water," she said, cradling the infant in one arm, while with her free hand she scooped up a small cup of water from the bucket and forced a little of it into the child's mouth. Lilli spooned some of the vegetable soup simmering on the stove into a dish and set it on the table.

"God bless you, pretty lady," the Slovakian woman said in Yiddish as she sat down on a stool and began to gulp down the steaming soup. Mother asked Lilli to fill a washbasin with water so she could wash the baby. We watched the infant come back to life, kicking and enjoying the sensation of the warm bath. Then Mother lifted the infant out of the basin, wrapped her in a towel, and left the kitchen, taking the baby with her.

The woman began to talk. "I had no time to take anything. I just ran."

"Where were you being sent?" Lilli asked.

"Only God above knows and I hope he is keeping track of what is taking place."

"Piri," Mother said, as she came back into the kitchen, "I want you to take this woman and the baby over to Mrs. Silverman's. You know where she lives?"

"Yes."

Mother had dressed the baby in one of Joli's old dresses, and she held, along with the baby, an armful of Joli's baby clothes and diapers. She handed the child back to the woman.

"You must leave here," Mother said to the woman, "but I'm sending you to a place where you will be safe for a while. It is a shelter that some of us set up. My daughter will lead you. Take off your head scarf and try not to look Jewish. We'll give you a hat."

After an emotional farewell and many mentions of God, we walked to the gate. Mother looked out to make sure no one was watching. "Piri, you walk ahead, and if somebody stops her, keep walking; you don't know them. After you've left her at Mrs. Silverman's, I want you to come right back. You understand?"

"Yes, Anyuka."

I walked with a normal stride several paces ahead of the woman. No one noticed us, and soon I was at Mrs. Silverman's gate, the woman with her infant still behind me. I hesitated a moment, then rang the bell. Mrs. Silverman appeared almost instantly, opening her gate just enough to let me through. I started to explain why I was there, but she interrupted, "Come to the point, child. What is it you want?" I closed my mouth and motioned the woman to come up. As soon as she got close enough, Mrs. Silverman pulled her into the yard and leaned out over the gate, checking both sides of the street. Then she pushed me out. "You've never been here," were her parting words to me. I walked home swiftly.

"Everything go all right?" Mother asked, turning from the stove to look at me as I came in.

"She is there. What is Mrs. Silverman going to do with them? Does she hide people in her house?"

"Piri, Hungary is the last place for them to run to, it is the last refuge. Don't you have any homework to do?"

I realized then that Mother was involved in things I knew nothing about, and was reminded of how much she was like Babi; when she changed the subject, that was the end of the discussion. But I could not get that woman and her baby out of my mind, and sometimes when I thought or dreamed about her, the woman's face became Mother's or Lilli's.

In the following weeks I met other runaways on the streets of Beregszász. I learned to recognize them from a distance. Most of them were women, some older, some younger, but their posture showed that they were refugees. Their bodies drawn in almost to a curl, they moved fast, yet hesitated a few seconds, scanning the space around them. Sometimes they asked me for help and sometimes I went over and whispered swiftly in Yiddish, "Follow me at ten paces behind, and I will take you to shelter." I didn't bring them home, but had them follow me straight to Mrs. Silverman's. She no longer asked me what I wanted when she opened her gate, but beckoned the runaway behind me in as she searched the street, and then pushed me out with a whispered "Be careful."

One day when Iboya was with me, we recognized a boy of about seventeen as a runaway. I went up to him and whispered in Yiddish the words that I had used with the others, but instead of falling in behind me as I turned away, the young man grabbed me, his hunched shoulders instantly relaxed, and he broke into a stream of Yiddish sentences. Iboya joined me alongside of him, and we started to walk three abreast.

"Mother said not to talk to them, just to walk them over," I protested.

"Nonsense," said Iboya, "if anyone stops us, we'll just pretend he's a friend of ours. And if we act natural, nobody will stop us."

The young man, speaking animatedly in Yiddish, told us what had happened to him and to all the other Jews rounded up in Bratislava. He was surprised that Iboya and I did not know about the new anti-Jewish laws in Slovakia, defining who was a Jew. "They are rounding up Jews all over Slovakia," he said.

"Who are they?" we asked.

"The Hlinka Guards—they are Slovak volunteers in the SS—the Gestapo, Hitler's secret police. Some of them used to be our friends, but the Gestapo gave them boots and uniforms and made them feel important. Some can't even read or write their own names . . ." He sighed. "Anyway, in our town alone they rounded up close to a thousand of us since the law came out."

"What do these new laws say?" I asked.

"That Jews are stateless unless our forebears were residents before 1868. They keep chasing us from place to place, then ask us to prove that we have lived in one place for over seventy years."

"Where are they taking these stateless Jews they round up?"

"To German-held territories."

"What are they going to do with them?"

"I'm not sure. That's why I ran away. They say all sorts of horrible things like slave labor and massacres. Who knows what the truth is? Germans, they will do anything to the Jews."

As we reached Main Street, Iboya asked the young man, whose name, he told us, was Jonathan, to lower his voice. "Too many people on this street," she said. When we were a few houses away from Mrs. Silverman's gate, I walked on ahead.

"So it's you again," said Mrs. Silverman, drawing back inside her yard after having opened the gate for me. I waved Jonathan in.

"Thank you," he whispered, as he hurried past me. Walking home, Iboya and I hardly spoke.

One afternoon, on the eve of Simchas Torah, I came home to a big celebration. Mother pulled a postcard out of her apron pocket and handed it to me. "Your father made it back to the train without getting caught. He is alive," she exclaimed. There were only a few lines of writing on the card: "All is well with my men and me. I miss you and the children. No address for a while, we'll be on the move. With love I kiss you. Ignac."

"They must be near Russia," Mother said.

Mrs. Gerber, Judi, and Pali arrived just as Mother and Lilli finished preparing a batch of doughnuts concocted from a mixture of flour and cooked pumpkin.

"How nice to see you," Mother greeted the Gerbers. "We are about to have a treat." Mrs. Gerber took a postcard from her purse and gave it to Mother, who read it and then smiled at her. "Dear Charlotte, just in time to celebrate the holiday. God is still keeping us in mind." Handing it back, Mother pushed the plate covered with doughnuts toward the Gerbers as they sat down around our crowded kitchen table. "Be careful," she said, "they are still very hot in the center."

"My, that's good," said Mrs. Gerber as she bit cautiously into the puffy pastry. "Whatever is it made of?"

"I have been stretching the flour with all sorts of tricks I learned from my mother. For these, I mixed mashed pumpkin into the flour. But I also use potatoes or squash or carrots; it just depends on what I have on hand and what I am baking."

"Babi once made fish balls without fish," I offered. "She had all her ingredients prepared and was waiting for Michael to bring her his catch. Then it got so late that she couldn't wait any longer. I remember what she said: 'Fish or no fish, I have to go on with the Sabbath.' So she mixed all the other ingredients together, rolled the mixture into balls, and simmered them in the usual broth. 'Babi, how can you make fish balls without fish?' I asked her. 'The same way I make them with fish,' she answered. But what really surprised me was that they tasted like real fish balls."

"You see, Charlotte, what a good teacher I had," Mother commented with a laugh.

"How is your mother?" Mrs. Gerber asked.

"Rozsi still writes and tells us that they are managing, and my mother sends us whatever she can spare."

"I don't know how much longer the Stern brothers can bring us baskets from Komjaty," Lilli said. "The fact that they look like two Ukrainian peasants helps them to keep from getting caught. It's their activity in the black market that keeps their families alive."

I usually went to the train station when Rozsi wrote that one of them was coming. The first time Mother sent me on this errand alone was during the summer. She had told me that if anyone asked questions about who gave me the basket, I was to say that the man got right back on the train and that I didn't get a good look at him.

"Why can't Iboya do it?" I had asked fearfully.

"Because you are younger and smaller and won't be noticed as easily."

When I met the 7:30 a.m. train from Komjaty that morning, my heart was pounding in fright. Shimi Stern was the third person off the train. He spotted me instantly and put down his bundles, hunching over them as though he were looking for something. As soon as I got close, he straightened up and stepped away, leaving a basket on the platform. I picked it up and he walked right past me with no sign of recognition. The basket was very heavy; a man's tweed sport jacket was pulled through the handle and covered the contents. I hiked it up on my right arm and let the weight rest on my hips as I walked home. Mother, waiting at the gate, took the basket from me, and together we walked into the kitchen. After Mother had hung the sport jacket in Father's wardrobe, she emptied the contents of the basket on the table—jars filled with lekvár, raspberry jam, and egg yolks; a small sack of barley and one of yellow dried peas. After that first time, meeting the train every few weeks became a game.

Lilli's remark about the possibility of the Stern brothers' being caught was prophetic, though. A few days after the Gerbers' visit, I came home from school to find Shimi in a gray prison uniform and a policeman sitting on our porch, each engrossed in a plate of food. Mother was standing over them on the kitchen threshold.

"Come, Piri, you look hungry; I'll fix you a plate,

too," Mother said nonchalantly as she walked with me into the kitchen.

"You mustn't ask questions," she said as she handed me a plate of mashed potatoes covered with giblet gravy. We both went back to the porch, and I sat down next to the men.

Shimi looked up from his empty plate and smiled. "How is the schoolgirl?"

"Are you in jail?" The question slipped out before I had thought.

"Yes, Piri, I'll have to wait for a trial. I was allowed a visit to have some of your Mother's good cooking."

I was about to ask another question when I remembered Mother's warning, so I just nodded at his comment and continued to swallow my potatoes in silence, noticing, though, that there were slivers of chicken on the police-man's plate. When the policeman finished, he stood up and motioned to Shimi, who stood up also. Then he hand-cuffed Shimi; they both thanked Mother for the dinner, and the policeman led Shimi away.

As soon as they had disappeared, Lilli came up from the back yard.

"What do you think will happen to him?" she asked Mother.

"I think that they'll let him go. They can't lock up everybody who has a few extra ration coupons."

"If they caught me with one of the baskets, would they put me in jail, too?"

"No, but I think this policeman would have liked to take Lilli to jail." Mother and Lilli both laughed their grown-up laughs.

"Why did you give the policeman meat?" I asked enviously.

"So that he'll be tempted to bring Shimi for another visit."

Shimi did come again a few days later, but this time he came alone.

"How did you get out?" Mother asked.

"I talked myself out."

"You ought to give it up, Shimi," Mother said.

"And do what? I have no other way to make a living."

He asked for his sport jacket. Mother put a plate of soup on the table for him and told me to get the jacket from Father's wardrobe. When I returned with the jacket and handed it to Shimi, he pushed the soup dish aside and asked me for a pair of scissors. I got the one from Mother's sewing basket; he took it and proceeded to cut open the lining around one of the sleeves of the jacket. Pulling out the shoulder pad, he looked up to make sure that he had our attention and called to Lilli, "You are the one who loves to bake, how would you like some coupons for flour?" Lilli came into the kitchen as Shimi opened the shoulder padding, exposing the small blue and white coupons. "How much would you like? Ten kilos?"

Mother drew in her breath. "Shimi, you can't afford to be so generous."

At Mother's comment, Shimi laughed and winked at me. "You earned it for bringing the jacket here."

"I insist on paying you the going price," Mother said.

"Rise, you have paid me a hundred times over."

Lilli took the coupons, stuck them inside the cover of her book, and gave Shimi a kiss on the cheek. In the winter that followed we were all grateful to him for that extra flour.

11

Iboya started to spend more and more time away from home. She would go to her Red Cross meetings and afterward stay out with other teen-agers. I missed not having her there with me while I did my lessons.

One day, walking to school, Iboya confided that she did not go to her Red Cross meetings every time she said that she was going there. She had been attending Zionist Club meetings with our aunt Lujza. She asked me if I wanted to go to a meeting with her some night. I wanted to go with Iboya and to be with Lujza and her friends, but I did not like to lie to Mother; I knew that she would disapprove, feeling the Zionist work was too dangerous for us.

"I'll think about it," I said.

"We'll tell Mother we're going to the cinema," Iboya continued, assuming that I had agreed to go. I didn't say anything.

A few nights later, Iboya told Mother that she was taking me to see *The Little Colonel* with Shirley Temple. We left the house and walked to the fur store where Lujza worked. She was waiting for us, and we walked quickly to the meeting place. As we went into the courtyard on Langel Street, it was just turning dusk, but inside the courtyard it was dark. Looking about, Lujza urged, "Follow me, and step inside immediately." She went down the path to the last house and rapped on the door in code. It opened, we rushed in, and the door closed behind us.

Inside, the big crowded room was a jumble of excitement. Most members were the same age as Lujza—in their twenties. Some called "Shalom" to us, others talked excitedly in small groups, and still another group in the right corner was singing along to a banjo. Lujza introduced us to many of her friends; "my brother's daughters," she said.

The room quieted down. Lujza pulled out some papers from her large handbag and read the reports of the last meeting. Then a man got up and spoke about some of the things that were in Lujza's report: numbers of families, cities, dates, boats, money. While he spoke, Lujza took notes. When he had finished, people started to ask questions, and discussions began. Lujza kept writing. When the discussions were over, a young man with a violin got up and started to play. As people gathered around him, a serious-looking young man whom Lujza had introduced as Shafar Joska came over and started to talk to Iboya. I suddenly noticed how grown-up and pretty Iboya was. Her face, flushed pink, was set off by her long, wavy blond hair, and her amber-colored eyes sparkled. As they talked, Shafar watched her attentively.

We began to sing "I'll See You in Palestine"; the tempo was almost too fast for the violinist, but he made his bow hop on the strings as he plucked on them with his fingers. The grim faces of the crowd relaxed and became more animated as the songs continued.

I wondered what Babi would think of this scene. I was pretty sure that she would disapprove. "Jews should behave like Jews," she would say, "without fear or hostility." The Jews in this now-swaying, smoke-filled room had, I felt, much fear and hostility in them. But their excitement was brief; too soon the violinist stopped his playing and wiped the sweat off his face. The group dispersed to start putting on their coats in silence. The meeting was over, and Shafar walked us home.

A week later, on Sunday, Lujza dropped in at our house for one of her infrequent visits. After a brief exchange of polite conversation with Mother, she went out to the back yard to join Lilli, who was in her usual seat under the walnut tree reading while the children played in the sandbox. As she spoke with Lilli, I imagined their conversation and guessed that she was trying to convince her to join the Zionist Club.

After Lujza left, Lilli came to the porch where Mother and I were braiding some onions to dry for the winter. "Here, Lilli," Mother said, handing her a string, "you help me while Piri does the beans in the kitchen. They are on the table, in a bowl," she said to me.

"I feel sorry for Lujza. She is crazy about children, and there she is wasting her years with politics," I heard Mother say to Lilli before I had finished shelling the first bean.

"How could she marry even if she wanted to?" Lilli asked. "All the men are in the army."

"She's older than you are. She should have married long ago," was Mother's comment.

"Are you still annoyed with her for siding with her mother against Ignac when he wanted to marry you?" Lilli countered.

"They never have forgiven me for taking him away from them. They objected to the marriage because I was a widow with small children and he was so young. But they would not have liked anybody who married Ignac."

"Well, it must have been nice to have Ignac at home. And you must admit that it is unusual for a young man to marry a woman who has five daughters. But you are so beautiful," Lilli said, laughing. "I can see why Lujza and her mother had no chance once Ignac had seen you."

Mother laughed, too. "Well, you were very stubborn about marrying Lajos when you were only sixteen. I never thought of it until now, but was it because of me and Ignac? After all, you were thirteen when we got married."

Lilli paused before answering. "When you sent me to Komjaty to stay with Babi, I half-thought you were trying to get rid of me. That is one of the reasons I married Lajos—to have a man of my own."

"Have you ever been sorry?" Mother asked softly.

"No, we needed each other."

Absorbed by their conversation, I had not shelled the beans. When Mother came into the kitchen, she noticed this and said, "Are you sitting here dreaming again? Get busy. I want to store those beans." She hung the garland of onions over the stove and went out to the garden to see what else she could find to harvest.

The following week, I stayed home from school because of a sore throat. Mother left the house in the morning to go to Mr. Kovacs, and when I had finished breakfast I went out into the back yard to find Lilli. Sitting down on the swing near her chair under the walnut tree, I asked her if she had thought about going to the Zionist Club with Lujza.

"No," she answered, "I don't think I would like it."

"I liked it."

"When were you there?"

"One night with Iboya. We told Mother that we were going to see a Shirley Temple film."

Lilli looked at me in amazement. "You two do lots of things you keep from Mother and me, don't you?"

"No," I said, "just that time. I haven't gone to a meeting since, and Iboya is busy with her Red Cross and War Aid training program. But I guess she still goes with Lujza sometimes. You would really like it, Lilli. They are all around your age and they sing Hebrew songs and dance the hora. But they also do important underground work with refugees."

"I could not do that work. It depresses me too much."

"Are you sad now?"

Lilli straightened up in the chair and smiled at me. "Not really."

But I wasn't convinced and ventured again, "I think you should go with Lujza. Mother always tells you that you should spend time with people your age."

"She would not like my being with Lujza and her friends."

Just then the mailman stuck his head through the open gate, and Lilli jumped up and ran toward him. I did not move, but heard him say, "I think I brought you what you've been waiting for," as he handed her a postcard.

"Oh yes, thank you." Lilli stood and read the card while the children clustered about her. "Is it from my daddy?" asked Manci.

"Yes," Lilli said as she read the card over and over. I took the children back to the sandbox and left her alone.

Finally, Lilli looked up and called us in to lunch. Mother came home just as we sat down. Lilli handed her the card and Mother commented, "See, everything is fine; you didn't have to worry about Lajos."

Lilli smiled. Mother sat down at the table, and Lilli handed her a cup of tea and served us our soup.

"How did it go?" she asked Mother.

"Mr. Kovacs gets more difficult every time."

"Did you get the money from him?" Lilli questioned again.

"Half of what he had been giving us. Well, I guess it will pay for the rations."

Lilli had been spending more and more time on the bread lines. Often, after she stood in line for over an hour, the store would run out of bread. We had the same problem with other staples. The half kilo of butter a week the seven of us were entitled to was hardly ever available, and it was almost impossible to get milk or eggs. The sugar coupons were about the only ones that could be redeemed.

Mother worried about not being able to get milk for the children. The Stern brothers did not come from Komjaty very often now.

Mother was still able to bake bread from the small supply of flour that she had, but she could not use the bread oven in the yard because of the suspicions of the neighbors. She awakened at dawn on the mornings that she baked and used the oven in the kitchen stove, stretching the flour with whatever starchy vegetables she had on hand. She also spent a lot of time gathering food for our meals, and put in long hours peeling and chopping at night so that she could cook while the stove was on in the morning. We were running out of firewood, with little hope of replacing it.

Since Lilli was now spending most of her time with us, Mother had convinced her to give up her apartment.

"We'll put your furniture in storage until Lajos comes home. With the food and the firewood situation, we are better off as one household," she said.

Lilli was unhappy about it at first. But then she said, "I am tired of being a gypsy. Half my things are here, and half are there. I guess it's just as well."

"With the money you save on rent, you'll be able to visit Lajos in the spring," Mother said.

After Lilli had moved in with us permanently, she and Mother managed to get some coal to keep the fire going and to cook with for the winter. Even though the kitchen stove smoked and the fumes were unpleasant, we got used to the discomfort—better that than being cold.

Then Mother thought that she might be able to provide milk for the children by buying a goat and keeping it in the empty woodshed. She knew a farmer outside of town who had been a customer at the store for over fifteen years, and thought that she could convince him to sell her a goat. She took all the money she had and Iboya and me with her on this venture out of town, leaving Lilli to look after the children.

Mr. Baltar was in the barn as we approached in the dusk of a November evening. We saw him through the open door as, with a pitchfork, he was spreading clean straw under his horses.

"Good evening, Mr. Baltar," Mother said. "Could I speak to you for a moment?"

"Who is out there?" the farmer called.

"Mrs. Davidowitz, from the shoe store. I have something urgent to ask of you."

"If you came here to talk to me, it must be pretty urgent." He put down the pitchfork and came to the door with his lantern. He smelled of the barn. Standing on the threshold, he raised his lantern in mid-air and looked down on Mother.

"I don't get many callers out here. What is it you came for?"

"It is the need for milk that brought me here. I have three small children at home and can't get milk for them. I'd like to buy one of your goats."

"Don't you know your zoning laws? You can't keep goats in the middle of the city."

"I don't live right in the middle of the city. Our house is more toward the edge. I have a perfect plan to keep him where no one will notice."

"What about your neighbors?"

"They've always kept a pig. I have an offer you can't afford not to take."

Mr. Baltar started to laugh, and his large body shook. "You certainly are a persistent woman, aren't you?" He waved his lantern at Iboya and me and asked, "Are those your little children who need milk?"

"No, those are my two big girls. They will help me get the goat home." She handed Iboya her purse and walked past Mr. Baltar into the barn, waving to us to follow her. On the barn floor at the right, the white goats stuck out like patches of snow lying about.

"Which one gives a liter or more a day?"

"This is a bad time of year to buy a goat. The spring is better."

"I need one now," Mother insisted. "My youngest is not yet two years old." She walked around in the semi-darkness, examining every goat's udder. "This one"—she pointed—"how old is she?"

Mr. Baltar was amused. He started to laugh his hearty laugh again. "You did not ask me the price."

"I'll give you twice her worth. How much is that?"

Mr. Baltar walked over to Mother and rested his heavy arm on her shoulders. He looked into her face, swinging up the kerosene lamp in his free hand. "Your husband is off for a while?"

"Yes, he is at the Russian border."

Slipping his hand down Mother's back, he turned to look at Iboya and me. "You can't walk a goat through the streets; I'll bring her myself on my wagon next Wednesday."

"It has to be at night, and I will need some feed and some straw."

"Hold it, hold it; we haven't agreed on a price yet. It will be two hundred pengö for the goat and twenty-five more for the feed and straw. Feed is expensive and hard to get."

Mother moved out from under his arm. "I have the money," she said, taking her purse from Iboya.

He took our address from Mother. "I'll be by on Wednesday when it darkens," he said as he patted Mother's rear. Then he waved us goodbye with his lantern.

"Men! And their conceit!" Mother said. Now she was laughing. "What ideas they must have. Well, we'll have milk for the winter, and if we are careful, we can stretch the coal through these cold months."

Mr. Baltar delivered the goat at dusk on the following Wednesday. As Mother led the way to the woodshed with all of us walking behind, I heard him say to her again, "You certainly are a very determined woman." With reluctance he left after the goat had been installed in her quarters and the feed unloaded from the wagon. We all helped to bring the sacks of feed to the woodshed and, when we had finished, stood and admired the goat. She had a round white body and thin limbs. Her well-shaped head was dotted by several black markings, which Lilli called her beauty marks. Her large black almond-shaped eyes had a dreamy look. Her ears pointed straight up, and down from her chin hung a smooth white beard.

Manci laughed as she noticed the goat's beard. "A lady goat with a beard," she exclaimed.

"Ladybeard," said Lilli, "what a name. That's what we'll call her. Ladybeard."

Slowly the children—Manci, Sandor, and Joli—approached the goat, and then hesitantly they began to pet her. Lilli took a few chunks of hay from the feed and let the goat eat it from her hand. Each one of us, except for Mother, then took a turn at feeding her. The children were delighted.

"It tickles," Manci giggled as Ladybeard's big wet tongue licked her small hand.

In the next few days our routines expanded to include Ladybeard. The children ran out to the woodshed right after breakfast to feed the goat and to pet her. At the end of the day, they returned to the woodshed to pet her good night.

Mother's attention was more practically focused. To her, Ladybeard's udder was of primary importance. She saved all of the vegetable peelings, which she cooked well, seasoned, and mixed with the grain husks of the goat's feed, giving Ladybeard rich nourishment. The goat thrived and even surpassed Mr. Baltar's promise of a liter of milk a day. But to all of us, even Mother, Ladybeard became more than just a source of milk and cheese. She provided us with a new interest, and we all cared about her well-being and contributed to her comfort.

In the weeks that followed the coming of Ladybeard, Mother and Lilli worked side by side preparing winter provisions. Somehow they were able to fill a large box in the kitchen with potatoes. They put up carrots and parsnips in wet sand for soup greens and dried several batches of noodles, which they stored in sacks. Lilli moved to Mother's rhythm now that she was in the house all day, but she still liked to take walks to the tobacco store, where she bought the newspaper, listened to the radio, and leafed through paperback novels.

*　　*　　*

For breaks, Mother and Lilli would sit and listen to the news on the radio. On a cold December day I came to join them in the kitchen, where they had moved the radio because it was the only room in the house that was heated. Mother held up her hand, signaling me to be quiet. "America has entered the war," she whispered. Her face paled and her eyes darkened as she listened intently to the urgent voice. This announcement shocked me. America was so far away. America, the land of hopes and dreams, where we were supposed to take refuge. What would happen to my uncles and cousins? Would they have to go to war?

"Oh whose side?" I asked as the announcer finished.

"With the English and the Russians, against the Germans, of course," Lilli answered, as she got up and turned off the radio. Mother remained seated, with a stunned expression on her face. "America in the war," she said over and over. I could tell that she was thinking about our family in America.

12

A week before Christmas vacation, Iboya and I walked home from school together. Chilled by the raw wind that threatened snow, we anticipated a warm kitchen and the usual chatter between Mother and Lilli. But we opened the door on a scene very different from the one we had expected. Mother sat in a chair near the stove, her face white, her eyes swollen from crying, her chest laboring with exhausted heaves. Frightened, Sandor and Joli stood by her helplessly.

"They came with Lajos and took Lilli," she said to us without expression.

"And Manci, too," Sandor added with tears in his eyes.

"They did not have to take Manci," Mother said. "I begged and pleaded for them to leave the child. They didn't listen. I would have given them anything, anything at all to leave my grandchild. What could they want with a

baby? She'll just be a burden to them. Maybe without her
. . . But now, nothing can be done. My poor Lilli, what
will become of them?'' Mother got out of the chair and
started to pace the kitchen. She walked around us and the
tables and chairs, waving her arms. Her voice hardly
audible, she spoke in a hoarse whisper. Iboya and I stood
watching her cry, and we felt as helpless as Sandor and
Joli. They now looked to us for comfort. Iboya and I eased
Mother back into her chair, and I picked up Joli, who was
shaking with cold and fright, while Iboya cuddled a bewil-
dered Sandor.

"This kitchen is freezing,'' Iboya exclaimed, and leaving Sandor's side, she started to poke at the few sparking
coals that remained in the ashes. After a while, Mother's
chest stopped heaving, and she half-dozed in her chair.
Then she sat up, looked at us, and said, "Feed the little
ones and all of you go to bed.''

We stirred and finished cooking the forgotten mushrooms on the top of the stove. "It must have happened
early in the day if the soup was only half-cooked,'' Iboya
observed.

"How did it happen?'' I asked Sandor.

"There were two policemen. Lajos' hands were tied.''

"Handcuffed?''

"Yes, I think so. Lilli and Manci went off with them.
Manci was crying, and Lilli was fighting with Mother.
Mother tried to take Manci from her.''

We fed the children and cleaned up. Mother was still
sitting in her chair half-asleep. Iboya locked the door and
we lay down with the children, falling asleep ourselves.

We did not go to school the next day. Iboya went out
and came back with our family physician and friend, Dr.
Feher. He gave Mother a powder and finally succeeded in
getting her out of the chair and into bed.

"What was the excuse they used?'' he asked her as he
helped her into the bedroom.

"Two counts: political sabotage against the Hungarian
army, and his citizenship was not in order. They said that
he was not a good Hungarian. Can you believe it, Dr.
Feher, calling Lajos disloyal and untrustworthy?''

"What is he supposed to have done?"

"They claimed that he said something against the Hungarian government. Someone made a report. Then when they went to check his papers, they found something wrong there, too."

Dr. Feher shook his head in sympathy and, after Mother was in bed, told us that she would be herself again, up and about, in a day or two. We knew that we would have to stay home from school and take care of the children until she was back to normal.

The next morning I got up early, dressed, and went into the kitchen, and there was Mother, standing at the stove, attending to things in her usual way. She told me to wake Iboya and get ready for school, that she was feeling better. The tone of her voice, firm and quiet, both convinced and cheered me, and I did what I was told.

The next day, at breakfast, she told us that she must go to Salánk to tell Lajos' parents what had happened. "I don't want to tell them in a letter, it's not the kind of thing you write to people about. I must go myself, so you girls will have to stay home from school until I get back." She made the fire and stirred up some corn mush for breakfast. Then she rushed into the bedroom, dressed, and came back. "The train leaves at 9 a.m. and I must not miss it."

"When will you be back?" Iboya asked.

"Either tonight on the ten o'clock train, or tomorrow night at the same time. I want to try and go to Komjaty to see Babi and Rozsi." She kissed us all, told Iboya and me to take good care of the children, and went out the kitchen door.

Iboya and I prepared ourselves to manage without Mother for the next two days. The children made few demands for attention; on the contrary, they were subdued. They seemed to have understood that a radical change had taken place in our home. Lilli and Manci, both constant companions to them, were gone. Sandor withdrew into himself, seldom speaking to any of us. He played in silence, but occasionally I overheard him whispering to an imaginary playmate. Joli was just starting to pronounce words other than our names, but she did not receive from us the enthusiasm that

Lilli had given to every new sound she uttered. She often called Lilli's and Manci's names, and kept looking for Mother, going to the door every so often and opening it as though she had heard someone knock. Joli's expectations, though, were met by emptiness, and she went back to her solitary playing in disappointment. Sometimes she went over to Sandor and began to mimic his actions and follow him around the house. When the mood struck him, he stopped what he was doing and played with her. But most of the time he played alone.

As the day progressed, I kept wishing for a visit from the Gerbers. But they did not come, nor did anyone else. Iboya and I spoke little to each other. We did the chores, watched the children, and when the day was over, went to bed ourselves. I fell asleep thinking about everything that had happened since my return from Komjaty more than a year ago. I woke to a rustling sound and saw Mother standing on the threshold of our bedroom. "It's all right," she whispered. "I'm home. Go back to sleep."

She didn't tell us very much about her visit to Salánk, only that she had been unable to get to Komjaty to see Rozsi and Babi. Over the next weeks, though, I began to notice a change in her manner toward people. She seemed less generous, more suspicious. Our mailman, Mr. Lakatos, could always count on a hot cup of broth in the winter and on a cold drink in the summer. He came in one afternoon, a week after Mother had returned from Salánk; I was in the kitchen helping her as Lilli used to. He had come to tell Mother the latest news from the Russian front. Instead of the usual friendly greeting and steaming mug of broth, Mother gave him a curt "Good day, Mr. Lakatos, have you a letter for me?"

"I wish I did," he had answered, "especially since I've heard the bad news about poor Lilli and her—"

"No need to be concerned," Mother interrupted, "it was all a mistake and they soon will be home again."

Mr. Lakatos put his head down and began to fumble with his mailbag. He straightened up, gave the bag a pat, and headed toward the door. "Well, I better be on my way to tend to my job, Mrs. Davidowitz. Good day to you."

After he left, I looked at Mother in surprise.

"If they aren't willing to help, I'm certainly not going to let them gloat over my misery," she said. And we continued our dinner preparations in silence. I remembered Babi's words, "You are fooling yourself. They are neighbors, but only your own can feel your pain." I felt sad to see Mother's bitterness in accepting the final separation from former friends and neighbors. Mrs. Gerber came to visit on New Year's Day and we all sat in the salon, listening to the conversation between her and Mother.

Mother told Mrs. Gerber about Mr. Lakatos. "He heard about Lilli from the neighbors. They talked about it, but nobody came to answer my cries for help the day they took her, and nobody has come since," she said.

"They are all concerned for their own safety," Mrs. Gerber replied. "They have no firewood and are short on rations. The men are away, and the Germans are running their country."

"Their country?" Mother exclaimed. "I used to think it was our country, too. And what about my Ignac and your Gabe? Aren't they serving in the army?" Mother was angry.

"Did you find out any more about Lilli and Lajos' transport?"

"No, I couldn't."

Mrs. Gerber said, "I think you should stop worrying about them. They will be all right with the money and jewelry you gave them. Thank God you had the presence of mind to do what you did."

"I just grabbed everything I had and put it into Lilli's coat pocket. I would gladly have given all of it to the police if Lajos had let me try to bribe them. Instead, he cried like a little boy and begged them to let both Lilli and Manci stay. And Lilli insisted that she would not be separated from Manci. 'We're staying together,' she kept saying. I took the chance that the police would see what I was doing because they stood over us all the time even while Lilli stuffed a few things into a suitcase. I was very careful and waited until they turned to answer something Lajos said. Then with the coat and the money and jewelry in the wardrobe I threw what I could grab into the coat pocket, and when I helped Lilli on with her coat I whispered to her in Yiddish about the things in the pocket. Who knows if the police took it or if she got a chance to use it."

My mind wandered away from Mother's description of the scene that by now I had heard several times. I began to think about the jewelry she had given to Lilli and wondered if the garnet earrings Babi had given me had gone into the coat pocket. But I didn't dare ask. I had visualized myself wearing those earrings with silk dresses when I grew up. Those dreams were beginning to seem foolish, and sometimes not being able to fantasize about growing up depressed me. Judi said that the war would be over by the time we grew up. But I was not sure that things in our house would ever be normal again.

13

One day in mid-January, Mother came to school with the little ones to get Iboya and me. That morning she had received a telegram from Lajos' parents telling her to be at the telegraph office at 3 p.m. to receive their telephone call. Iboya went home with Sandor and Joli, and Mother took me with her to the telegraph office. The man behind the glass wall at the desk told us to sit down and wait until we were notified that the call had come. Mother kept biting the knuckle of her fourth finger in anticipation. "They would not be telephoning unless they had an urgent message. God only knows what I am about to hear," she said to me. I looked at some of the other people seated around us, and they also seemed restless, frightened, and nervous.

"Did you ever talk on the telephone before?" I asked Mother.

"I once did in Budapest," she answered, "when I was a young woman. I called my brother at his office."

I was excited by the thought of speaking to someone who was two hours away by train from us. "Will you let me listen?" I asked.

"Yes," said Mother, "if it is possible. I don't know how things will be arranged."

Then the voice from behind the glass wall called, "Mrs. Davidowitz, your call is ready in number 6."

Mother jumped up in confusion, not knowing where number 6 was. I pointed to a booth and followed her to it. She did not seem to remember how to hold the receiver, putting first one end, and then the other, to her ear. When she had it right she said, "Hello, hello," into the strange-looking mouthpiece. "Yes, it is I." Her face drained of color as she listened. "Yes, yes, I have it. I'll leave tomorrow. Goodbye." She replaced the receiver on its hook and then rummaged in her bag for a pencil, found one and took it out, pulled the telegram out of her pocket, and held it against the wall of the booth while she wrote on it. Then she replaced the telegram in her pocket.

"You didn't let me hear anything," I said.

"I'm sorry, I forgot, and then they called the time."

"What did they say?"

"Let's get outside, and I'll tell you."

Once we were outside, the cold January air restored the color to Mother's face. "Lajos sent them a letter from Poland. He wants somebody to come for Manci. She has the whooping cough."

"Are you going?" I asked her.

"Tomorrow."

"How will you go? You can't go by train."

"I'll have to."

"What if . . ." I started to say, the fear beginning to thump in my chest.

"I have to go." Mother cut short my imaginings.

On the way home, Mother stopped at the fur store where Lujza worked. "Go in and tell her to come out," Mother said. "I don't want to go in looking like this."

I walked in and Lujza saw me immediately. Excusing herself from a fashionably dressed woman who was trying on a gray Persian lamb coat, she came over, bent down to my level, and asked quietly, "Is anything wrong?"

"Mother is outside," I answered, "and wants to talk to you."

"I'll have to ask my supervisor for permission to leave the store. You go back outside and wait with your mother."

She came out a few minutes later, wearing her pony coat unbuttoned. Mother whispered to her and showed her the telegram with the notes she had made. Lujza kissed Mother's cheek and said, "I'll be at your house between eight and eight-thirty this evening." She went back inside, and Mother and I walked to the shoe store.

"You stay here, outside; I'm going in to see Mr. Kovacs," Mother said to me. I peered between the shoes in the window display as Mother followed Mr. Kovacs around, trying to talk to him. The two people in the store were staring at her. I saw her remove her headscarf and adjust her hair with her hand. She cornered him at the door to the stockroom. I could see his impatience as he listened to her; finally he went into the stockroom and came back a few minutes later with a piece of paper, which he handed to her. She stuffed it deep into her coat pocket and took her leave by nodding to the staring customers.

Once outside, she took out the paper and carefully unfolded it. "Twenty pengö! He knows that I can't even buy a one-way ticket with this."

Next we stopped at Dr. Feher's office and sat down in the waiting room with his patients. One of them turned to Mother and asked what was the matter with her.

"It is my little girl," she said, indicating me with a nod of her head, "she has very bad cramps. I think it is her appendix." I doubled over to illustrate the pain of the cramps.

When Dr. Feher opened the door leading into his examining room, Mother jumped up. "It is an emergency! You must look at this child right away!" He led us into his examining room and closed the door. Mother pulled out the telegram and handed it to him. As he read it, she said over and over, "I must go. I must leave tomorrow." When he finished, he looked over at her and she took out the twenty pengö. "This is what Mr. Kovacs gave me. I had to beg for our money. Can you imagine? What a world we are living in! I'm so ashamed that I had to come to you."

Dr. Feher took out a few bills from his pocket, then went over to the bookshelf behind his desk, took down a book, opened the front cover, and removed the bills that were there. He came back to Mother and handed her the money.

"Here, you'll give it back when you can." Then he poured some medicine into a small bottle and wrapped it up. "One teaspoon every four hours. Good luck." He opened the door and we went again through the waiting room, Mother holding the small bottle of medicine in her hand.

Lujza arrived at eight-thirty accompanied by two strangers, a man about Father's age and a younger woman about Lilli's age. Lujza introduced them as "the artists." "They will need a place to work," she said to Mother, who led them into the salon. The young woman removed the plush table cover from the round table, folded it up, and carefully put it down on a nearby chair. Both of them took from their pockets an assortment of ink bottles, pens, papers, stamps, scissors, and erasers, which they placed in the center of the round table. Then they sat down, ready to work. Lujza rummaged through a box of old photographs that Mother had taken out of the wardrobe. They were still working when Iboya and I went to sleep.

"What are they doing all this time?" I whispered to Iboya in the darkness.

"Making Mother a passport. In case she is stopped."

"Why does it take so long?"

"It has to be perfect. She will be passing through German-held territory."

"Do you think it will work?"

"They do it all the time for the Zionists."

The next day I hardly recognized Mother when she left to take the afternoon train to Poland. With a heavy black shawl covering her head and shoulders, she looked like a peasant woman. Below the shawl hung a heavy cotton skirt, and on her feet were old leather boots like those the peasant women of Komjaty wore. Over her arm she carried a market basket. Iboya kept Sandor and Joli in the kitchen so that they would not see Mother leave. When I came back from bolting the gate after her, I asked Iboya where Mother had found the clothes she was wearing.

"At Mrs. Silverman's," Iboya answered.

"What did Mother put in the basket?"

"Food. All trayf. She even had bacon-grease sandwiches. I wonder where she got them," Iboya mused.

"Will she eat them?" I asked in surprise.

"I suppose she'll do everything she has to do to be accepted as a peasant woman."

"If any of the neighbors saw her leaving the house, I'm sure they thought she was someone from Komjaty," I said.

That night before we went to bed, Iboya and I double-bolted the door. Once we were in bed, we talked late into the night. Lujza stopped by the next evening to see if we were all right. "If she does not come back by tomorrow afternoon, one of you come to the store and let me know," she said. Iboya and I were prepared for a second long night of staying awake, when, a little before midnight, there was a tap on the window over our bed. We both jumped up in fright, not daring to pull up the shade. But then we heard Mother's voice through the glass, "Iboya, Piri, open the door."

We ran out in our nightshirts and asked, "Who is it?" to be sure it really was Mother's voice we had heard before we unbolted the door. She answered us in an impatient tone, and we quickly opened the door. We expected to see Manci, too, but the only thing Mother had with her was her empty market basket. Once we were all back in the kitchen, she collapsed into a kitchen chair, her body sagging in exhaustion. Iboya rekindled the dying fire in the kitchen stove and put up some tea. Mother kept rubbing her numbed fingers until they uncurled. Then, removing her boots, she went to work on her toes.

"It was freezing on that train, and it is much colder in Poland than it is here. Nobody has any firewood. Everybody is freezing. They hardly have anything to eat and they can't think about anything else—just firewood and food. My problem could scarcely interest them. Maybe if I had brought some extra food and firewood with me in a suitcase, they would have been more interested; my money couldn't buy them what they needed." She stopped rubbing her toes and sat up.

Iboya handed her Father's large mug filled with steaming tea into which she had poured a little rum from the special bottle kept for guests. Mother took a few quick sips and then rested the mug on her knees. Her face relaxed as the tea warmed her, and the heavy shawl slid from her shoulders as her chest heaved. "And nothing was accomplished!" she said.

"You did not find them?" Iboya asked.

"No, I was too late. They left that morning. I should have left the same night I got the message. I might have found them."

"But how could you?" Iboya interrupted. "You needed papers and the money."

"I also wanted the medicine from Dr. Feher," Mother added. "But what good was any of it? Manci is sick, and I left the money and the medicine in the hands of strangers. Who knows if they will even bother to look for Lilli. Well, they did put me up for the night and took me back to the train in the morning. They risked their lives just for that. So I guess they earned the money. And they did keep Lilli, Lajos, and that poor, unfortunate, innocent child. They surely took a big chance on that. They could have gotten themselves into plenty of trouble harboring deportees. At first they believed they were just political refugees. That alone was taking a chance, but even after they found that Lilli and Lajos were Jews, they still kept them another night. But Manci's cough got worse and they were afraid that someone would hear her. I guess I can't blame them. They live in constant fear. The pro-German Poles are everywhere and walk into houses unannounced. They said they admired my courage."

Mother drew a deep breath and continued, "I slept with one eye open and my boots on. And then a friend of their son, in uniform, stopped in just before they took me to the train. They introduced me as a relative visiting from Slovakia. But the way he looked me over, I know he didn't believe them. I was afraid to move, afraid that I would give myself away, like poor Lilli. I want you girls to listen to this so that you'll remember it. They managed with some money that Lajos gave them to get a fresh egg for poor Manci. Lilli cracked the egg on the edge of the bowl and carefully pulled the shell apart to examine the yolk for blood spots. She poured it from one half shell to the other before scrambling it, never realizing that only a Jewish woman does that. And there they stood—that old Polish couple—watching her, and they realized that they were harboring a Jewish family. The man told them that they would have to leave immediately. Only Lajos' pleading and Lilli's emptying her pockets, no doubt, made the couple consent to their staying one extra night. I saw the garnet earrings in the woman's ears when I arrived, that's how I knew I was in the right house." Mother glanced in my direction. So that was where my earrings had gone, I realized with a pang. "They promised to look for Lilli and Lajos after I left. The whole country is a caravan of soldiers and refugees."

"How will they find Lilli?" I asked.

"I don't know. If it were only Lilli and Lajos, I'd worry less. But with a sick child on their hands, God only knows!" Mother went on talking in the same rambling way until she fell asleep in her chair.

When I came home from school the next day, Mother was working in the kitchen and Mrs. Gerber was there, sitting and listening as Mother told her of her trip. I went over to the little ones who were playing quietly in their corner and, offering to read them a story from one of my books, took them into the bedroom. I couldn't bear to hear again about Mother's failure to find Lilli. Mrs. Gerber left at dusk; by then Iboya had come in, and we all went back into the kitchen to help with supper preparations. Just as we finished eating, someone knocked at the door. I opened it to admit a worried-looking Lujza. She came in quickly, saw that Mother was there, handed me her coat, and looking relieved, said to Mother, "Good. I hoped that you were home. And what happened? Did you find Lilli? Is Manci here?"

Mother began to clear the table. "Sit down," she said to Lujza, "and I'll make you some tea. I was going to send Piri over to the store this afternoon to tell you I was back, but Mrs. Gerber was here, and I forgot. I'm sorry. I know that you were worried. But the trip was a big failure."

Lujza sat down and so did Mother as Iboya and I continued to clean up. Mother began again to tell the story of her trip, and Lujza sat silently during the recital, nodding from time to time. Finally, Mother stopped talking, but she was in tears.

"You did the best you could, Rise," said Lujza softly. "And maybe the Polish couple did go to look for Lilli; they would know far better than you where to look."

"I know, I know," said Mother. "That is why I did not try to go any farther. After all, I have other children to think about, too."

"Well," Lujza repeated, "you did the best you could. We all did."

We didn't hear anything about Lilli for several weeks. Then, one afternoon in late February, Mother received a written message telling her that Mrs. Kertes' son Miklos was home on leave and wanted to see her. That evening after dinner, Mother left Iboya with the children and took me with her to the Kerteses' house. Miklos' wife, Mari, a tall, thin, cold-looking woman, answered our ring. She showed us into the salon and then left the room, returning a few minutes later with Miklos. He came over to Mother, who stood up, and he kissed her hand. Mother sat down again and Miklos remained standing, pacing up and back, as he spoke. He told Mother that he had seen Lilli at a train station in Poland a few days ago; he had been getting ready to board his train when he heard someone call his name, and he recognized Lilli's voice. They had after all, as he said, grown up together. She broke out of the line she was in and started to run toward him, but was stopped by a guard and forced to go back.

"They were also waiting for transport," Miklos said. "These trains don't stop. Everybody is on the move. Night and day. They even load people into freight trains."

"Was she alone?" Mother interrupted.

"No, there was a man with her. And she kept yelling to me, 'Tell my mother you saw us, tell my mother you saw us.' "

"And the child. Was there a child with them?" Mother's voice became tense.

"Yes." Miklos nodded.

"Are you sure?"

"Yes, the man was holding a child. I saw them again as our train moved past them. I did not see the man's face, but he was standing next to Lilli, and he was holding a child, a girl."

Mother tried to ask Miklos a question about what else he had seen in Poland, but Mari interrupted the conversation at that point to say that she felt Miklos had spoken enough.

"He has been traveling for days and is very tired. I think you'd better go now."

We stood up, and Mother thanked Miklos for bringing her Lilli's message. As Mari walked us to the door, she told Mother that Miklos had been on the Russian front and had seen some dreadful things.

"That is where my husband last wrote from," Mother said.

"I hope you get him back home," Mari replied, "and please don't tell anyone that you have been here."

On the walk back to our house Mother repeated to herself several times, "The child is alive; she is alive." But words failed to affect her spirits. Her face remained ashen, her voice low and heavy with sadness.

14

In April 1942, after months of probing and letter writing, Mother and Mrs. Gerber received letters telling them that Father's troop was in a Russian prison camp. However, no word came from either of the men. Mrs. Gerber and Mother spent more and more time trying to cheer each other up, using any excuse for a break in their worried existence.

Then we lost Ladybeard. One afternoon in May, a knock sounded at the kitchen door. Mother opened it to see two strange men standing on the threshold.

"Are you Mrs. Davidowitz?" one of them asked in a formal tone of voice.

Mother's answer, a breathless "Yes, yes," indicated to me that she hoped these men had come with news, either of Lilli or of Father.

"We are inspectors from the city housing bureau," the taller of the two men said solemnly, "and we have come to investigate a complaint that you are keeping a goat on the premises. This is, as you know, a strictly residential neighborhood! No animals other than dogs and cats are allowed!"

"You don't have to investigate," said Mother, lingering a little over the last word. "I admit that I have a goat in my woodshed. But, gentlemen, this goat is not bothering anybody, and she provides milk for my children. I'm sure you are reasonable men with children of your own. You can't blame a war mother whose husband is in a Russian prison camp for trying to feed her young children, can you?"

"We are inspectors from the Housing Department, and we have nothing to do with conditions of war. Where is this goat?" the taller man demanded.

"I'll take you there, and you can see for yourselves what a gentle and quiet animal she is. She could not disturb anyone." Mother led the men off the porch into the yard and returned a few minutes later for the milking bucket. "I'm going to milk her at least; she is so full that she can hardly walk."

"Don't let them take her away," Sandor pleaded.

"They won't listen to me," she answered him gently. Then she turned and left the kitchen, carrying the milk bucket. Sandor and Joli ran out after her. I grabbed our coats and followed them.

When I got to the woodshed, I saw Joli had thrown her arms around Ladybeard's neck. "She is mine," she screamed at the two men who towered over her. "She is mine!" I saw them exchange glances. Mother pulled up the milking stool and proceeded to milk Ladybeard while I struggled with Joli to leave Ladybeard long enough for me to be able to put on her coat. Sandor stood at the wood-shed entrance and looked at all the somber faces without giving a hint of what he felt. I had always been struck by the way Sandor, even as a small child, could hide his feelings. Was this, I wondered, what was meant by the expression *being a man*. I looked at the two inspectors' faces. "Stone," I said silently to myself. Mother and Joli had enough expression for all of us; both of them were crying uncontrollably. But the only sound we could hear in the woodshed was that of the squirts of milk rhythmically swishing into the bucket. When Mother finished, she picked up the bucket and started to walk off, not saying another word to the men.

"Do you have a piece of rope?" the shorter man asked her.

"In the kitchen."

All of us followed Mother into the kitchen. She put the bucket down on the kitchen table and tried again to persuade them not to take Ladybeard. "Couldn't you just forget that you saw her?"

"We have to do our job, lady," the shorter man snapped at her. "Just give us the piece of rope, and we'll be on our way."

Mother started toward the drawer where she kept string. Joli grabbed at her skirt; Mother picked her up, opened the drawer with her free hand, took out a long, frayed piece of rope, and held out her hand. As the shorter man walked over to take the rope, he passed the opening into the salon, glanced through it, and saw the radio.

"Didn't you know that you were supposed to turn those in last January?" The other man walked into the salon and unplugged the radio. He wrapped the cord around it and put it under his arm. Then he joined his companion, who was standing on the threshold, holding the piece of rope. Without saying another word, they walked off.

Mother put Joli down, closed the door after them, and stood facing us with her back against it. After a few minutes she walked out of the house, went down to the gate and bolted it, came back into the kitchen, and picked up Joli, who was still crying.

"What will they do with Ladybeard?" I asked.

"Send her into the wilderness with their sins, I suppose."

"I don't understand."

"It doesn't matter," she said as she went into the bedroom.

In the fall, a few days before school was to open, we heard that Jewish children would no longer be permitted to attend the public schools. Mrs. Gerber decided to give Iboya, Judi, and me lessons in Hungarian, German, and history. Iboya and I went to their house every morning, coming home at lunchtime. We had to walk past the schoolhouse on our way home, at the time that the other children were in the yard on recess, and it felt strange looking in from the outside to see them practicing gymnastics.

By October, the Jewish teachers, who had been barred from teaching in the public schools, opened a makeshift school in the Sunday-school room of the big synagogue on Main Street. The students in the room Iboya and I were assigned to ranged from fifth to tenth grade. The teachers at first attempted to teach all the school subjects, but soon gave up in despair and decided instead to concentrate on math, reading in Hebrew and Hungarian, and Jewish history.

It was here that I discovered Gari Weiss, who was almost three years older than I. His family was one of the wealthiest in town, and owned the big house in back of the brick factory. I sat and watched him in class as much as I could, and decided that I liked him best on the occasions when he wore a white shirt, which made his dark complexion look very manly and set off his sleekly combed back hair. Instead of doing my lessons, I would write notes to Gari, asking him to meet me in various places, and then tear them up. He walked home from school through the same streets that I did, but Robi Berg was always with him. He also played tennis with Robi on the tennis court in back of the Weisses' mansion. Judi and I often watched them play tennis, scheming unsuccessfully to attract Gari's attention. Iboya teased me about my crush on Gari, but Judi understood because she, too, had a crush on a clerk in the bookstore. Hari was sixteen, and she talked to him about books.

"Doesn't your mother mind?" I asked Judi the day she told me that Hari had eaten supper at her house. "He is so much older than you are, and he isn't Jewish."

"Those things don't bother my mother. She is modern," Judi answered very emphatically.

Whenever Judi told me how modern the Gerbers were, she made me feel uncomfortable—as if they were better than we were. I couldn't help wondering what she would think if she ever met Babi. Or what Babi would think of her. When I had first told Judi about Komjaty, her comment was, "Someday I'd like to see that sleeping village."

"Those people are not sleeping," I had protested. "They work very hard."

"They are sleeping in history," she had insisted. "They've let progress pass them by. They think and work the same way their ancestors did. They don't read the newspapers. They don't even know what goes on outside their village."

"My Babi reads the newspapers and she knows all about Hitler."

"Then she should have listened to your mother and gotten out of there."

"But she can't leave her land and all her animals."

"She is holding on to her land in false hope. I heard my mother talk about her. My mother said that your grandmother thinks that by holding land in Hungary, she is part of Hungary. No Jew is a part of the land he lives on and even owns unless that land is Palestine."

"But you and your mother think that you are Hungarians."

"Not really."

Judi had a way of confusing me, and sometimes it seemed to me that she enjoyed doing just that. "My Babi is very smart," I continued on that occasion. "She reads Hebrew, Yiddish, Ukrainian, and Hungarian. Even the rabbis in Komjaty respect her and ask for her opinions on things."

"Rabbis," Judi had interrupted sharply, "are not modern thinkers."

It was impossible to win an argument with Judi. When we tried to discuss a book we had both read, we realized how different our points of view were. And Judi would invariably comment, "You didn't read it with an open mind."

I did get ahead of Judi in one thing, though. I began to menstruate before she did. I felt it start one day while I was sitting in class at our makeshift school, and at recess I ran to find Judi and tell her. In spite of our having discussed menstruation many times, I was quite scared and shocked by it.

"Would you go and tell Miss Solomon that I went home with a stomach ache?" I asked Judi.

"No, I won't," she answered. "We must both go to her and tell the truth." She took my hand and led me over to the corner where the teachers sat at a table drinking their tea. I tried to pull free, but she held on so insistently that I felt embarrassed to run away.

"Miss Solomon," Judi asked as we came up to the table, "could Piri and I see you for a moment? It's urgent."

Miss Solomon left her place at the table and walked down the corridor with us. Then she stopped and waited for one of us to speak. Judi waited a moment for me to speak up, but I was too shy.

"Piri wants to be excused for the day," she said finally. "She just started to menstruate."

Miss Solomon's mouth opened in surprise. Then, looking from Judi to me, she said, "Piri, you are excused, and you don't have to come back until you feel fit."

"May I walk home with her?" Judi asked.

"Yes, Judi, you may. Be careful, both of you," and having said that, she turned away from us and went back to the teachers' table. We got our books and left.

On the way home, Judi asked a dozen different questions about what it felt like to be grown-up and to menstruate. I was grateful when we reached home and Mother, in her silent and efficient manner, took over.

15

Iboya did not find the makeshift school agreeable. She could not concentrate in the unruly and noisy classroom and developed frequent headaches. Because of them, she had lengthy discussions with Mother about the possibility of her quitting school and finding work. But Mother insisted that she had to stay in school at least until she was sixteen. Mother also pointed out that it would be next to impossible for a Jewish girl to find work. One Friday afternoon in early spring, as Mother and I were cleaning the fish which Mr. Schwartz had just brought, and Mr. Schwartz sat at the table sipping hot broth, Iboya came in from school, her face white and her eyes narrowed in pain.

"Another headache?" Mother asked.

"Yes," she answered, setting her books down, and asking Mother for some aspirin.

Mother handed her the aspirin bottle from the cupboard, and then exclaimed, "I know you are restless and that school isn't fun. But you are too young to quit!"

"I don't see why," Iboya began again, repeating an

argument I heard her use several times. "We don't learn anything there, anyway. Nobody is interested in learning about wars their grandfathers fought in, when there is a war right outside our doors."

"How old are you?" Mr. Schwartz interrupted, looking directly at Iboya.

"Fifteen."

"What would you like to be doing instead?"

"Lujza has been taking her to the Zionist Club," said Mother before Iboya could answer Mr. Schwartz's question. "And I know that she is very impressed with their mission."

So Mother knew Iboya's secret! Iboya's face flushed deeply as she, too, realized that Mother had not been fooled by her different excuses for coming in so late from her Red Cross meetings.

"Did Lujza tell you?" she asked Mother in a haughty tone.

"No, she did not have to tell me. I was a revolutionary, too, at your age. I know all the signs."

"Do you think you would like to come to work for me in the store?" Mr. Schwartz interrupted.

"What could she do in your store?"

"I need a cashier. Somebody I can trust."

"You're not permitted to hire a Jewish clerk."

"She could be what she is—a friend's daughter helping out. I could use her on Thursdays and Fridays, the busiest days. With meat impossible to get, all the Jewish women, like you, need fish for the Sabbath meal. I would find ways of compensating Iboya for her work. Credits at other stores. And I wouldn't charge you for Friday's fish!"

Mother laughed. "You haven't charged me for the fish in quite a while. I hope you're still keeping an account."

"But with Iboya working for me, she can work off the account. Of course, she'll have to get used to the smell of fish."

We had never gotten used to Mr. Schwartz's smelling of fish. We hated to sit next to him during the Friday evening meals he shared with us, and Mother had begun to invite

him even more often since Lilli had gone. His empty
sleeve had upset Lilli.

I had once heard Mother tell Lilli, "Losing his arm was
a blessing in disguise. Mr. Schwartz is the only Jew in
town still permitted to run his own store, and he still gets
his pension payments as well."

"He gives me the shivers," Lilli had replied. "He's a
constant reminder of the war."

"That is how his wife must have felt. She ran away
after he came home from the World War. Stupid woman.
Didn't she realize how lucky she was that he came home?
There are worse fates than having a man with one arm."

At the time of that discussion, Lilli had put on her coat
and walked out, saying she was going for the newspaper.
Apparently, she did not care to hear any more about Mr.
Schwartz and the war.

Now Mother turned to Iboya and said, "It sounds like a
good idea to me. I'll get you excused from school on
Thursdays and Fridays. What do you think?"

"I'd certainly like to try it," Iboya said with enthusiasm.

"It's not exactly what I had in mind for my girls, but
there is a war on, and working is always respectable,"
Mother concluded.

So Iboya went to work in the fish store. She had to wear
a rubber apron there because of the splatter of fish scales.
When she came home on those nights, she would heat pots
of water and immerse herself in a tub of suds, trying to get
rid of the fishy odor. I could still smell the fish in her hair
while we lay together in bed, but I never mentioned it.

After Mother's return from Poland, Lujza became a
frequent visitor at our house. She and Mother seemed to
dissolve their prior antagonisms as they sat at the kitchen
table in the evening, sipping herb tea, plotting possible
means of getting Etu home from Budapest. One night, as
they discussed Etu's situation and Rozsi's, Mother suddenly asked Lujza if she could get any information on
Father's prison camp in Russia, and how to get a letter to
him.

"Rise, I wish I had the means. After all, he is my

brother. You should hear what goes on at home. My mother thinks that the Zionists are magicians. She wants me to find out not only about Ignac, but also about Srul and his wife in Russia and my brother-in-law in Rumania. I wish the Zionist underground were half as powerful as you and my mother would like them to be. As a matter of fact, with the new law of restriction on travel and the Americans not sending us as much help and money as they used to, almost everything has stopped. No, I'm afraid it's almost all over. Our main mission—to get Jews out to Palestine—is finished. Whoever did not get out by last December is stuck. Nor can we do a lot of the things we used to do. We had to give up our regular meeting place, and we are being watched, the really active Zionists like me, I mean. And if the police pick one of us up, they do not punish just the one individual; the entire family receives the same punishment—deportation to Poland. It just happened to one of our most active agents. He and his whole family—father, mother, wife, and children—were deported. Who can take it on his conscience to bring such a fate on his family?'' At this point, Lujza stopped talking.

Mother got up to brew her a cup of tea, scraping at the bottom of the can to get out the few remaining leaves. When the tea had set, she poured a cup for Lujza. Then, on a sudden impulse, she moved quickly to the cupboard that held her precious last bottle of rum. She took the bottle out and uncorked it. Lujza held her teacup while Mother gently tilted the bottle and splashed a small amount of the amber fluid to mix with the dark Russian tea.

"Have some, too, Rise," Lujza insisted. Mother hesitated for a moment, then placed the silver tea strainer over a fresh cup, poured some of the tea for herself, and added the rum. Their faces began to relax as they sipped the tea.

Lujza smiled. "Well, it looks as though the Allies are going to be able to chase the Germans out of North Africa."

"Africa," said Mother. "What good is that to us? What we have to hope is that the Russians get here before the Nazis take over completely."

Lujza looked shocked, but she didn't say anything. The

Communists, I knew, were anti-Zionist, and I was surprised to hear Mother say what she had said. But I didn't make a comment either. Lujza got up slowly, took her coat, said goodbye to us, and left.

Mr. Schwartz started taking Iboya with him to Porta, a small fishing village near the Slovak border where he met the fishermen as they hauled in their catch. They left at dawn on Thursday and Friday mornings and were back at the store by 9 a.m. to open the doors for the waiting crowd that had gathered. By noon the fish were all gone, and Mr. Schwartz had to close for the day. Sometimes the people who had not gotten any fish threatened to knock down the locked door. Iboya had to leave the store by the back way with her fish hidden in a piece of tarpaulin.

One Thursday evening, while we were eating supper, Iboya complained of a bad headache, and she seemed unusually tired and upset.

"I could tell Mr. Schwartz that I don't want you making the trips to Porta with him to get the fish," Mother said.

"You can't now," Iboya answered. "He really needs my help."

"He could take one of his other helpers."

"They are goyim and can't be trusted."

"Do you handle money in dealing with the fishermen?"

"That and . . ." Iboya stopped and cupped her hand over her forehead.

"You are now getting headaches from the fish?"

"It's not the fish. It's those people," Iboya burst out.

"What people?" Mother looked serious. "Tell me about it."

Iboya threw a worried glance in my direction. I was burning inside with anger. Ever since she had started working at the fish store, she had alienated herself from me. She had become too grown-up to confide in me. She had drawn into herself and lay silent in our bed, her eyes shut. But I knew she wasn't sleeping. "I don't care if you don't want to talk to me," I had said angrily.

"It isn't you, I can't talk to anybody," she had answered.

Now Mother stroked Iboya's hair. "It's all right," she

said. "Piri would never repeat anything she is told not to repeat. Not even to Judi." Mother gave me a warning look. I nodded my head in agreement.

"Mother, Mr. Schwartz hides people on his fish truck on the way back from Porta," Iboya said slowly. Mother's face grew white and tense. "You know, refugees," Iboya continued after a moment's pause. "This morning we brought in a woman with two children. One of them kept crying, she was so frightened under the tarpaulin."

"How long has this been going on?" Mother's voice was stern.

"Ever since I started to go there with him. He sits up on the box holding the reins, and I sit next to him riding backwards to watch where he can't see. If I see anyone coming, I throw the tarpaulin over the passengers. They have to stay under it until there is no one in sight; then they can come out for air. Today we had our first incident. A policeman on a horse stopped us and heard one of the children crying.

" 'My little girl is sick,' Mr. Schwartz said, 'I'm taking her to be looked at by a doctor.'

" 'No wonder she is sick,' the policeman laughed, 'lying with that stinking fish.'

"Mr. Schwartz pushed his papers into the policeman's hand and turned to me. 'I told you to pick her up and hold her,' he yelled. 'Why did you put her down there?' He slapped me, reached under the tarpaulin, pulled the screaming child out, and handed her to me. Next he reached under the tarpaulin again, pulled out a large fish, wrapped it in a piece of newspaper, and handed it to the policeman.

" 'Take this home to your wife. It was swimming two hours ago,' he said.

"The policeman gripped the fish in his gloved hand and handed Mr. Schwartz back his papers. 'I guess everything is in order,' he said.

"What if the policeman had looked under the tarpaulin and had seen the woman with the other child? I was so scared!"

"What happened to the woman and the children when you got back to Beregszász?"

"He usually drops me off with whomever we have with us on the corner of Tinodi Street, and then I walk them to Mrs. Silverman's."

Mother looked thoughtful for a while. "I am going to talk to Mr. Schwartz when he comes for dinner tomorrow night," she said finally, "and put a stop to this. It was not part of the bargain."

"But, Mother," Iboya replied, "there are so many people that need to be taken, and he can't trust anyone but me. I usually don't mind. It was just this morning with the child crying and his yelling at me. I didn't know what was going to happen. Mr. Schwartz really handled it very well by yelling at me, saying all of that to the policeman, and giving him the fish."

Now that I had heard Iboya's story, I felt very ashamed at my anger, and understood that she was only trying to protect me by not telling me anything. Still, I wished that she had trusted me enough to tell me. I could keep a secret, even from Mother, if I had to. After all, I never told Mother about Iboya's seeing Shafar whenever she went to the Zionist meetings. Somehow I had to make Iboya understand that. And I certainly wasn't going to tell Judi about what I had just heard. In fact, the idea of knowing something she didn't pleased me.

At dinner the following evening, Mother did voice her surprise to Mr. Schwartz at what he and Iboya were really doing in Porta, and she questioned the wisdom of letting Iboya continue to help him. But he managed to convince her that he could handle any other situation that arose just as well as he had the one yesterday. He really needed Iboya, he said. So Iboya kept on going to Porta to bring back refugees all through the summer.

That fall, a few days after our makeshift school had started its second year, I was in the kitchen helping Mother prepare our dinner. The door opened and Iboya, drained of color and energy, came through it, a newspaper tucked under her arm. Mother put down the tray of potatoes and took the paper from her. Her back stiffened as she read the headlines.

"Hungary is right in line with Czechoslovakia, Poland, and Germany in carrying out Hitler's orders against the Jews. They are all the same, and we are all Jews, and nobody cares." Iboya spoke in a bitter tone.

Mother threw the paper on a chair and turned back to the potatoes. Iboya took off her jacket, hung it up, and began to set the table. I took the newspaper from the chair and opened it. "JEWS MUST WEAR THE STAR OF DAVID."

The next morning, the town crier appeared at our street corner. He stood with his booted feet spread apart, the big drum hanging from a strap around his neck and covering most of his short body. His hands beat the drumsticks in furious rhythm. When the crowd around him had grown to about a hundred, he tucked the sticks under the drumstrap, and rolled out the scroll of announcements. Clearing his throat, he stretched out his neck and started to read.

"By the end of this month, September 30, 1943, it will become mandatory for all Jews in Hungary so defined by Article 270 to wear a yellow star sewn on the left side of their outerwear. A curfew will also be in effect. Jews may not leave their homes before 10 a.m. or after 3 p.m."

Iboya and I stopped listening and left the crowd, but we did not continue on our way to school, where we knew little teaching would be done that day. Walking through the streets aimlessly, we came to Tinodi Street and stopped to watch an organ grinder. As he cranked the handle at the side of his box, playing the melody of "Sorrento," a large colorful bird danced on the flat surface in rhythm to the tune. After the song was finished, the man passed around his hat, and received a few coins. Iboya and I were embarrassed that we had none to give, and walked on slowly. We met a family of refugees from Rumania, a mother with two little girls about two and six years old. She told us they had been walking for days and could not find lodging. We took them to Mrs. Silverman. When we finally got home, we found Mrs. Gerber and Mother sitting on the porch. We told them about the Rumanian woman and her two children.

"A friend wrote to me from Budapest that there are over fifteen thousand Jewish refugees roaming the roads of

Hungary, and the government is pretending not to be aware of them," said Mrs. Gerber.

"But now, with the curfew in effect, and the Star of David, that will be pretty difficult," commented Iboya.

"My grocer heard that Horthy succeeded in rejecting the Germans' demands on enforcing the yellow star," Mrs. Gerber replied.

"What about the curfew?" I asked.

"It could be worse," said Mrs. Gerber.

But the curfew was related to rationing, Mother explained when she returned home from the market with an empty basket. "After 10 a.m., there is nothing left. Now we can throw away our ration coupons. They are of no use to us."

16

Late one night, we heard a knock at the door. Mother jumped out of bed, fumbling in the dark trying to get into her bathrobe. I could see her silhouette struggling with the sleeves. "Why don't you put on a light?" I asked. She did not answer.

"Who could it be at this hour?" I huddled up against Iboya and could feel her body shiver. I recalled the time Father jumped the train and knocked at our window in the night. I prayed, "Dear God, let it be Father or Lilli." Iboya and I got out of bed and joined Mother at the door. She called in a forced voice that did not sound like her at all, "Who is there?" The hoarse voice that answered sounded just as strange.

"It is I, Sanyi."

"Oh, my God! What has happened"

"It is Lujza," sobbed our uncle Sanyi outside the gate. Iboya and I stood behind Mother and watched in the moonlight. Mother unbolted the door with rushed, trembling hands. Sanyi passed through and tried to talk, but he could not stop sobbing. His fingers held the collar of his black coat up around his neck. Mother put an arm around him and led him into the kitchen. She switched on the light, looked at him, and then cuddled him in her arms.

"You poor boy!" Sanyi put his face on her shoulder and stopped sobbing after a few minutes, picked up his head, and looked into Mother's face with red, feverish eyes.

"Lujza is dead!"

"How? When? Because of the Zionists?"

"No. She was accused by her supervisor of stealing money from the store. She came home from work very depressed. They had told her not to come in any more. She would never steal anything. They lied." He began to cry again.

"But how did she die?"

He drew a deep, racking breath and continued. "The train. We heard the screeching of the train. It was the night train from Miskolc. Father and I ran out to see what made the train come to a stop outside our house. We have heard the trains pass all these years, but never heard one stop before it got to the station. There was a big commotion, and a crowd had gathered. 'A woman threw herself under the wheels,' a man told us. 'The train ran right over her.' Father and I moved through the crowd and saw two train-men lift a body wrapped in a blanket onto a stretcher. In the dark, we could only make out that it was a female form. So we started to walk back toward the house. When we got to the front door, there was a policeman with some papers about to knock. 'Mr. Davidowitz?' he asked.

" 'Yes, can we help in any way?' Father answered. He thought that since ours was the nearest house to the accident, the policeman wanted to ask us for help.

" 'Do you have a daughter named Lujza? There's been an accident.'

" 'I know. We've just come back from there, but what has my daughter to do with it?' Father and I were sure that Lujza had gone to a Zionist meeting.

" 'Would you please come with me?'

"Father and I walked back to the track. They held a

lantern over the stretcher and uncovered the body. 'Could you identify the victim?' the policeman asked. We saw it was Lujza, but neither of us could speak. Her head was flattened out; her body, mangled; but we knew it was Lujza. She had been wearing her pony coat. It was all torn. Father told them to put her body in the barn. He wanted to talk to Mother before we brought her into the house. Then he told me to come here to tell you.'' Sanyi's face quivered all the while he was talking, and his hands shook. Mother cradled him and rocked him again in her arms. She only came up to his shoulders, but Sanyi leaned over to rest his head at her neck, so they were both on the same level. Iobya and I stood looking at each other, and then we started to cry.

"Iboya, make the fire. Piri, get the brandy," Mother snapped, her voice almost normal again. She sat Sanyi down and brought a blanket from the bedroom to wrap around his shoulders.

"You are staying here till morning," she told Sanyi. "You have seen enough for one night."

"I can't. I must go back to help," he protested.

"There is nothing you can do. You are lucky you were not picked up coming here. We are not allowed to walk the streets at this hour. When it gets light, you and I will go together. Do you have your papers on you?"

Sanyi looked at his coat. "I'm wearing Father's coat. I thought it was mine." He reached into the breast pocket and pulled out a black folder. "I have Father's papers."

"You are lucky; they have been picking more people up at night then they used to. We'll wait until morning. There is nothing to be done now and your parents know where you are."

Mother poured out some pear brandy and handed the glass to Sanyi. His hands shook as he brought the glass to his lips and drank. After he handed the empty glass back to Mother, Iboya and I sat down on either side of him and held on to his arms. Sanyi did not push us away.

Sanyi left our house with Mother the next morning. When Mother returned in the afternoon, she told us that Lujza's funeral would take place the following morning and that Iboya would go with her while I remained at home with Sandor and Joli. In a way, I was glad that I did not have to go to the funeral or to the cemetery afterward. I suddenly remembered that Lujza was only a little older than Lilli.

After they returned from the funeral, Iboya told me that hardly anyone had come to see Lujza buried. No one from the Zionist organization had appeared. Mother said they probably hadn't come because they were afraid. Nobody believed the story about Lujza's stealing the money. The police had found out about her Zionist work, and she was aware of it. Her suicide was her way to save her family. Iboya said that Mother was the only one who didn't cry. Grandma Davidowitz kept fainting and they had to hold her up.

"She was a brave girl," Mother repeated over and over. I kept picturing Lujza standing in her pony coat alone in the cold night waiting for that train. And then the harsh metallic sound filling her ears just before. I had to agree with Mother. Lujza was a brave girl. Thinking back about her, I realized that she was always very serious. At the Zionist meeting she didn't get caught up in the songs and the dancing as the other young women had. Instead, she kept busy with her papers and watched the others participate in the social part of the meetings.

After Lujza's funeral, Mother clamped down on our activities. "No more trips to Mrs. Silverman's. No more meeting the train from Komjaty. And no more going to Porta with Mr. Schwartz. I have to keep whatever is left of my family intact. The Germans are infuriated with their losses on the Russian front, and they will take that anger out on us!" She remained firm with Mr. Shwartz when again he tried to convince her to allow Iboya to continue with trips to Porta, and she even questioned letting Iboya remain as cashier in the fish store. But she finally yielded to necessity on that matter, and Iboya went on working at the cash register in the fish store Thursdays and Fridays, bringing home fish for our supper.

Shafar appeared at our house one snowy evening a few weeks later. He had just received papers to report immediately for work in one of Budapest's new ammunition factories, and he wanted to say goodbye to Iboya. Knowing that Iboya had been going to Zionist Club meetings, Mother accepted Shafar as Iboya's comrade. In fact, she seemed to like him. As we all talked about Budapest, she mentioned Etu, and he promised to look her up and to see what he could do to help her. Iboya walked out to the gate with him when he left, then came back into the house. She avoided Mother's questioning eyes, and said that she had a headache and was going to bed. I could tell from Mother's knowing look that she realized there was more between them than cameraderie.

Mother started scraping the bottom of her flour sacks. No food came from Komjaty that winter. A letter from Molcha explained why. The already meager harvest of 1943 had been confiscated for the war effort, leaving the farmers themselves only a tiny allotment. Babi's livestock, including the chickens, had been taken away from her. Even her plum trees and grapevines had been picked bare.

Rozsi's letters, however, were protective; she did not want Mother to worry. "We are managing very well," she wrote in all of them. She had stopped asking if there were any news about Lajos, Lilli, and Manci or any mail from Father. Mother had stopped sending us to meet the mailman at the gate and no longer waited anxiously on the porch every day at mail time. It wasn't that she thought they were lost. I often heard her discuss their whereabouts with Mrs. Gerber; together they speculated that Father, a war prisoner in Russia, had probably managed to contact his brother Srul, who, by now, had some political influence, having been such a devout Communist all these years. Mrs. Gerber kept assuring Mother that the money she had left with the Polish people must have been delivered to Lilli. Lilli couldn't take a chance on writing, she reasoned, because any mail coming to us from Poland would provoke suspicion.

I could not tell if either of them really believed what they were saying or if these conversations had become a ritual of their visits. Mrs. Gerber usually arrived at our house feeling very depressed.

"I just had to come today," she invariably said. "I could not contain my thoughts. My mind is going to finish me off; I can't deal with it all. And the children wanted to come."

Mother always found something to entertain them with, a quick vegetable soup or potato pancakes, or boiled noodles sprinkled with our home-grown chopped walnuts and a pinch of sugar. To Mrs. Gerber's constant amazement at her ingenuity, Mother replied, "I am a farm girl at heart." Our own vegetable garden provided many of these meals and supplemented our dwindling rations. Mother not only canned the vegetables, but also replanted the carrots and parsnips into boxes of moist sand and brought them into the house. This method kept them fresh and furnished new growths of tops to pinch for soup greens all winter long. Mother had also stored up sauerkraut, pickled cucumbers, and tomato puree, as well as a small barrel of salted herring made from the fish supplied by Mr. Schwartz. Mother was a wonder of resourcefulness.

Mrs. Gerber, not wanting to be on the receiving end all of the time, sometimes arrived with a gift from her house.

"If you don't stop this," Mother said, "you'll end up with an empty house."

"My house is no good to me full or empty," Mrs. Gerber replied. "You always cheer me up."

Judi, Iobya, and I never ran out of conversation, and Pali, Sandor, and Joli always seemed to be amused in their games together. Joli, now three years old, had grown into a beautiful little girl despite the hardship and grief surrounding her. She and Sandor became good company for each other and, looking at them together, I often remembered the way Sandor and Manci used to play with each other.

I never spoke of Manci in front of Mother. I could not bear the pain in her eyes at the mention of her name. Not even the absence of Lilli hurt as intensely as the loss of her granddaughter. She never stopped wrestling with the thought that Manci could have been saved. In a thousand ways, it kept repeating in her mind that she could have stopped them from taking her.

Sometimes when I woke up during the night and went into the kitchen for water, I found Mother sitting there in the cold. I would startle her by touching her on the shoulder and saying, "Anyuka, go to bed, the house is cold."

"I can't sleep," she usually replied.

At a loss to console her, I would get my coat, put it on, and sit down beside her, saying nothing. In this silent way we often sat together, waiting for a new day.

The winter snow was finally washed away by the rains of a new spring, and patches of green began to appear in the garden. The days grew warmer, and the sun dried the sandbox. Sandor and Joli moved out of doors to play. The walnut tree sprouted buds. Passover was approaching, and Mother quietly started the preparations. The tradition was so deeply ingrained that neither yesterday's sorrows nor the rapidly approaching Germans could alter the ritual. I helped Mother take down the Passover dishes and sweep out the chometz; every last crumb of bread from pantry and cupboard was collected and burned together with the straw broom. A few days before the holiday eve, she discovered a forgotten box containing Passover condiments. "I want to share these spices with Grandmother Davidowitz," she said to me. "You must take some to her." I left our house with her firm instructions to return immediately after I had delivered the spices.

When I arrived at the Davidowitz house, I had to knock on the gate several times before Sanyi, looking confused and anxious, came out of the house. He opened the gate to let me into the yard, but instead of continuing to the house, he stood with me in the yard.

"What are you doing here?" he asked.

"Mother sent these Passover spices to Grandmother," I replied, showing him the small box I was holding. "Are you having a seder?" I continued hesitantly, remembering their recent sorrow.

"Piri," Sanyi answered, "we are leaving the country.

Mother and Father have already left the house with a special messenger from the Juden Bureau. I am packing a few things before I meet them. The Germans are about to take over."

I must have looked shocked as I felt a great surge of panic envelop me. I took a deep breath and asked, "Where are you going?"

"I don't know. Lujza arranged everything before . . ." Sanyi stopped for a moment and then went on: "She even had Christian papers made for us, and I think she was planning to have them made for you, Iboya, and the children. Your mother already has them—from her trip to Poland to look for Lilli. I have to go." He took me to him and hugged me tightly. "Tell your mother to run, too," he said as he released me. I did not know what to say. I went through the gate and then turned to watch him disappear into the house.

"Mother," I said, when I returned to our kitchen, "they have no use for the spices. They are leaving the country. Sanyi said to tell you to run, too, because the Germans are taking over." Mother dropped the plate she was drying, which shattered into fragments at her feet.

"Did he say where they were going?"

"He didn't know. Lujza had arranged it all with someone at the Juden Bureau. She also had Christian papers made for them like the ones you have, and he said that she was planning to have them made for the rest of us . . ." Mother turned while I was still speaking and went into the bedroom. She began to gather up clothing to pack, but soon she abandoned the piles of clothing she had thrown on the bed. "Where could we go?" she said, shrugging. "You children have no papers, and it is two-thirty, almost curfew time." She went back to drying the dishes, and I asked, "What exactly is the Juden Bureau?" She explained, "It is an organization made up of prominent Jewish men. They act as our leaders."

Just then Iobya came into the kitchen carrying a fish wrapped in newspaper. "Did you hear anything?" Mother asked her.

"They say that Horthy has been locked up by the Ger-

mans and that a new government is coming into power.
Something about a take-over. The new government is
going to be more cooperative with the Germans. We have
to wear the yellow Star of David."

We put the light out early that evening but did not go to
sleep. Mother, Iboya, and I sat in the dark and listened to
every sound outside our window. Even in the darkness of
the bedroom, I could see Mother's face tense at the sound
of footsteps in the street or at the sound of male voices.

"You two are going to sleep in the summer kitchen
tonight. I put some bedding on the chair along with two of
my old dresses and two kerchiefs. I want you to look like
beggar women, so that if they do come they won't bother
you. Piri, you will unbraid your hair and hide it all under
the kerchief. Smudge your faces with ash from the stove.
Make yourselves as unattractive as possible. Soldiers after
a victory behave like animals. I remember that from the
last war, and these are Germans. So you must do as I tell
you."

"What about you and the children?" Iboya asked.

"They won't bother me, and they have no use for
children. Looting and young women are what they are
after."

After a while the fired died out, but we remained sitting
on Mother's bed with our clothes on. As the room grew
colder, we climbed into the bed and pulled the feather-
down coverlet over us. Listening to the rhythmic breathing
of Sandor and Joli made me drowsy, and I put my head on
Mother's shoulder. She kissed me on the forehead.

"Iboya," she then said, "take Piri and bed yourselves
down, but first do as I told you." We all got out of her
bed, and she lit a candle and walked us through the long
porch and into the summer kitchen, shielding the candle
from the wind with her cupped hand. She dripped some of
the wax onto the cold stove and made the candle stand
upright in it. "You must blow out the candle as soon as
you have finished. Move fast and get under the covers. Do
not make noise under any circumstances. You must remain
silent no matter what you hear."

I tried to hold on to her, but she slipped away after

turning the key in the door of the summer kitchen and disappeared. Iboya, following her instructions, moved quickly. She unbraided my hair, helped me slip one of the old dresses over my head, and then smudged my face with ash. "Tie the kerchief so that none of your hair shows," she said. Then I helped her to dress in the same way. We blew out the candle and got under the covers Mother had left on the bed, shivering from cold and from fright. Iboya turned toward the wooden plank wall and I curled around her as close as I could get, my ears keen all the while, listening to the shouting voices and the tread of boots on the ground, Iboya's breath, and the wind. Then I heard other sounds—scuffling and gnawing.

"What is that?" I asked Iboya in a whisper.

"Mice, I think," she answered and I tensed and snuggled still closer to her. The mice continued to chew on whatever they had found to eat, and I closed my eyes and held my breath as long as I could.

The next thing I was conscious of was light and the sound of the key in the door. Mother came in wearing old clothes, her face smudged, and a kerchief on her head hiding her hair. For a moment I forgot where I was and was startled by Mother's strange appearance. Then, seeing Iboya sitting up beside me dressed the same way, I remembered what had taken place last night. "You can come out now," Mother said, "things have quieted down."

"Did they come?" asked Iboya.

"They came," Mother answered.

"I heard them," said Iboya.

"They did not come into our house, but they were on our street."

Sandor and Joli laughed when they saw Iboya and me come into the kitchen. "You two look funny," Sandor said. Joli stopped giggling and her steel-blue eyes showed fear. She wrapped her arms around her small body and shook. "I don't like you this way."

Mother gave us a basin of water. "You can wash your faces now—there should be no trouble during the day, but any contact with the Germans will be dangerous. Yellow star or not, I don't want you to leave the house. Not until we see what happens."

By ten o'clock, Mother had changed into her disguise. Now, dressed as a peasant woman, wearing the same clothes she wore to Poland when she had gone looking for Lilli, she said to us, "Bolt the gate, lock up the house, and don't let the children out. I must run and pick up the matzos I ordered at the temple yard. Maybe I can pick up something else at the market next door as well, and then I'll come back. Tomorrow is the first night of seder."

"Don't you want me to come along to help?" Iboya asked.

"No, you are to stay in the house with Piri and the children."

After Mother left, Iboya told me that yesterday in the fish store she heard someone say the Germans had taken over Budapest.

"What will happen to Etu?" I asked as we cleared away the breakfast dishes. "Why did Mrs. Gerber tell Mother to leave her there, saying that she would be better off in Budapest?"

Iboya looked at me, started to say something, changed her mind, and continued to wash the dishes in silence. And as I continued to dry them, I remembered the time of the Hungarian-Ukrainian border war when the closing of the border kept me in Komjaty. In my mind, I could see Rozsi, Babi, and me sitting in the kitchen listening to the sounds of gunfire in the distance. I was so afraid, I wanted to run and hide. But Babi sat very calmly in her chair reading her prayer book. I looked to her face with each explosion; not once did she wince, but just kept on quietly reading the prayer. And the next day when I had seen the bodies of the soldiers floating in the Rika, and had run home to Babi, filled with fear and confusion, I remembered how gently she had calmed me. And when Grandpa died, she had come out of the bedroom and said softly, "God took him to Himself."

"Why did He take away my grandpa?" I had asked.

"Because we are all His," she answered. "We are only

here to do His work, and when we finish, He takes us back to Him.''

I thought then that God must be very selfish, but had begun to understand that Babi's strength came from inside her, from her faith. I tried to trust and to accept things the way she did, but I couldn't feel Him anywhere, especially not now.

17

Iboya's concerned voice interrupted my mind's wanderings. ''Mother has been gone for two hours. I wish she had let me go with her.''

''What do you think will happen to us now that the Germans are taking over? Will we become refugees, too?'' I asked.

''There is no other place to run. Hungary was the last country to give in to Hitler's demands about the Jews.''

Mother did not return until half-past one. She came in carrying a large brown paper package tied with string. Her face was white, her eyes murky and dark.

''Children,'' she said, ''the Germans are parked in our temple courtyard. They have taken it over as their head-quarters. I have just spoken to them. I conversed with German officers.'' She set the parcel of matzos on the floor and walked over to the chair. She did not look at us, but stared straight ahead as she continued to talk.

''As I came through the courtyard gate, they were asking if anyone spoke German. I could have pretended not to understand. I don't know what possessed me, but I said, '*Ich spreche Deutsch.*' Can you imagine me offering to help them? An officer waved me in and asked me to direct him to the Juden Bureau. I started to give him directions, but he said, 'Come in the car and show us.' I had no choice. He told me to sit in the front with the driver, and he sat down in the back seat. So I am inside a car and riding with two Germans. The officer sitting in the back asked me questions about the different places we passed.''

"Could you answer all his questions in German?'' I asked.

"Not very well, but he seemed to understand. He made me come into the Bureau in case he needed me to translate. I got some looks from the men as we walked in. I wasn't sure whether or not they recognized me. Mr. Hirsch welcomed us in as if we were important expected guests and pulled up some chairs for us. Once I heard Mr. Hirsch's German, I knew that they would not need me, but I sat and listened anyway.''

"What did you find out?''

"First they talked about where they would be staying and about provisions for the soldiers. Then the officer said that they had locked the old men at prayer in the synagogue and would release them for an agreed sum of money. Mr. Hirsch did not seem surprised. God only knows who is in there or how long they might keep them. They were sitting and discussing it as though it were a simple business transaction involving merchandise. Then they talked about dividing the city into districts. They studied a map, and looked at a list of names that Mr. Hirsch gave them, and the German officer put red marks on the map for each of the names. I couldn't follow the reason for the red marks. Then I jumped up from the chair and said, 'I must go home to my children.'

"The officer, whose name had been mentioned several times by then—von Heckendorff—jumped up, too, and shook my hand and said, '*Danke schön, Frau . . .*' and waited for me to supply my name. "Da-vid-o-vitch,' I said, giving it the Russian pronunciation. Thank God our name isn't Cohen or something like that, or I would have had to think very fast and lie. As it was, I did not look at Mr. Hirsch or at any of the other men. I left quickly. I ran all the way back to the temple yard, through the market, and ducked into the matzos stall. Mr. Heller could not believe that I had come to pick up the matzos.

" 'It is a dead giveaway,' he said. 'If they pick you up with them, they will know; your clothes will not help.'

"All the packages were stacked against the wall waiting to be picked up. They had finished baking and packing the matzos before the Germans got here. I put down my thirty pengö, picked up my matzos, and stepped right back into the marketplace. I waited by a stall for a few minutes, and when I saw that no one was nearby, I ran. Luckily, the Germans are so disorganized and worn out by last night's carousing that they are not yet aware of the matzos stall. But I saw some of the soldiers walking through the market, helping themselves to whatever caught their fancy, so it won't be long before they find out about the matzos."

Later that day, two yeshiva students came to ask for money to make up the ransom for the old men locked in the synagogue. Mother opened her purse.

"What is the ransom?" she asked.

"Twenty thousand pengö," one of the students replied.

Mother turned her purse upside down over the kitchen table. She smoothed out some bills and gathered up the change. "Twenty thousand pengö! I'm afraid that my seventeen pengö and change won't make much of a dent in that amount."

"We are also asking for jewelry and other valuables," the other student said.

"I have already given those things away," Mother replied, and the student left, thanking her for her contribution.

Toward evening, Mr. Hirsch came from the Juden Bureau. I let him in and Mother jumped as he came through the kitchen door.

"What are you doing out? It is past curfew."

"I am on special permission." Mr. Hirsch pointed to his white armband. "We just aren't getting close to the twenty thousand pengö demand, so we are going out ourselves, hoping to find people more generous to us than they were to the students."

"Clever, aren't they, the Germans, the way they have us following their orders," Mother commented bitterly. "You giving them names of important townspeople—working one Jew against the other."

"What choice is there?" Mr. Hirsch protested. "We hope that our appointments will give us some bargaining power—to ease the blow, so to speak. And what were you doing there today, dressed as a peasant woman? We weren't really sure it was you until you gave your name. What a chance you took! What were you doing out?''

"I have children. They need to eat," Mother said, walking Mr. Hirsch into the salon. They stayed in there and talked for a while. Mother came back to the kitchen without her pearl earrings. They were part of her features and she looked bare without them.

"You gave him your earrings!" Iboya, like me, had noticed their absence at once.

"That is all I had left to give," Mother said to us as she walked Mr. Hirsch to the gate.

The day of Passover Eve, Mother decided to send me over to the Gerbers to find out how they were. I was afraid to go.

"By myself?" I asked.

"It is broad daylight. It is three hours before curfew time and things have quieted down," Mother said. "You are still a child, they won't question you, but we will dress you up just in case." She sat me down and unwound my braids. Instead of the usual side part, she made a part in the middle of my head and rebraided my hair. Then she took the black peasant shawl and tied it covering part of my head and crisscrossed it under my arms with a knot in the small of my back. After surveying me a moment, she said, "Take off your shoes. Go barefoot. It is not cold. Once you start walking, you'll be all right. Skip to keep warm if you have to."

She gave a demonstration, skipping across the kitchen. She called Iboya in from where she sat in Lilli's chair watching Sandor and Joli at play in the sandbox. "What do you think?" Mother asked her after Iboya had come into the kitchen. "I am sending Piri to look in on the Gerbers. They would not dare to wander out of their house."

"Her feet are too clean. Otherwise, she looks like a peasant girl."

"Good. I would like to send them some of the matzos

for their seder, but I don't dare send her out with matzos on her.''

''They don't believe in Passover anyway,'' I said. But to make it just a little special, Mother brushed the white sprouts off four shriveled potatoes, poured some sunflower oil into a little flask, and tied it all up into a small bundle.

''They can have some pancakes out of them. I wish I had an egg. Don't tell them about my going for the matzos. Say we are fine and that as soon as things calm down, we'll get together. Don't go by Main Street near the synagogue. Take the long way. And you are to come right back! Rub some dirt on your feet in the yard; I'll be right out to give you a final looking over.''

Still apprehensive, but curious to see if Beregszász had changed, I let Mother push me through the gate. The sun was warm, and the chestnut trees lining both sides of our street were covered with tight buds ready to burst out into shiny leaves. The cement sidewalk, hard and coarse under my feet, felt strange. I had walked barefoot in Komjaty so many summers, but this sensation was different. I was a peasant child in the city. I wondered if Molcha would feel strange if she were walking here now, if she would stare at the colorful brick and stucco houses and look into the modern shop windows. Two German soldiers appeared with rifles on their shoulders, coming toward me. I knew that I could not look frightened. I kept walking at the same pace, and they passed by me silently.

Approaching Dr. Feher's house, I heard loud voices and, as I came closer, saw people all over the yard. I wandered into the courtyard and soon heard the reason for the gathering of the crowd. Dr. Feher was dead. German soldiers had broken into his house last night and violated the women—both his wife and his daughter. He could no longer bear to live, he wrote in a note, and then shot himself with a hunting rifle.

I was too confused to understand anything beyond the fact that Dr. Feher had killed himself. I continued on my way to the Gerbers'. I did wonder, as I walked, where all the people in Dr. Feher's yard had come from. There were so few people now on these once-busy streets. Then I remembered that tonight was Passover Eve, the first seder night. On this day, in other years, these streets had been filled with people scurrying about in preparation. And here I was carrying four potatoes to the Gerbers for their seder. Their lives, too, must have changed from what Judi had told me about the many elegant parties they used to give in Budapest.

When I knocked on the Gerbers' door, Judi opened it and stood, with hesitant eyes, holding the door ajar.

"Who is there?" called Mrs. Gerber in a frightened voice from inside the house.

"Come and see for yourself," Judi answered. "I almost didn't recognize you," she said to me. "Your disguise is perfect."

Mrs. Gerber came to the door and stood looking at me in amazement. "Come into the house, let's not stand here," she said, leading the way into the kitchen. Once we were all inside, she turned to stare at me again. "Did your mother dress you up this way?" she asked.

"Yes, she was worried about you and sent you some things to make potato pancakes with."

"I can't believe your mother. What an actress she might have been." Mrs. Gerber took the package from me. "She took such a big chance in sending you. Did you see anything on your way over here?"

"Yes, two German soldiers with rifles on their shoulders walked right past me. I must go home." I didn't think I should mention Dr. Feher.

"Can I walk her back part of the way?" pleaded Judi, reaching for her coat with the bright yellow star on the lapel.

"No, it is not safe for you to go out there with German soldiers on the street."

Judi slipped into her coat anyway. Mrs. Gerber grabbed her. "You are not going any farther than the yard."

"I want to talk to Piri for a moment," Judi said quietly.

Mrs. Gerber hesitated, then, putting on her coat, she led us out with Pali following behind her.

"I want to talk in private," Judi snapped. She pulled me toward the open gate.

"Stay inside and close the gate," Mrs. Gerber ordered. She turned and took Pali by the hand; together they went back into the house.

Judi waited until her mother had gone before asking, "What is it like out there?"

"There is hardly anyone on the streets. But I walked past Dr. Feher's house and he is dead. I wonder if we should tell our mothers. He shot himself. What does 'violated' mean?"

I was surprised that Judi did not answer me. She looked confused.

"The people in the courtyard said the reason Dr. Feher shot himself is that the German soldiers violated his wife and daughter," I explained.

"Raped," she said. " 'Violate' is a word the grownups use to confuse us. What they mean is 'raped.' "

I took her answer in slowly. "Did the soldiers come to your street, too?" I asked.

"No. Luckily, we live too far out of the main area. We heard from our neighbor that the hospitals are full of victims."

"They did not come into our house, but they were on our street. Mother was scared that they might . . ." I decided not to tell Judi about sleeping in the summer kitchen. "I really must go," I said.

Mrs. Gerber came running toward me from the house. "Take these to your mother," she said when she reached us at the gate. "I know that she will go through some of the rituals for the seder in spite of everything falling apart. These will dress up her table. And do be careful." She gave me a little package.

"Mother said we'll get together as soon as things quiet down," I said, walking through the gate.

As I neared the public-school yard, I saw German soldiers spilling out into the street. I did not know what to do. If I crossed to the other side of the street, they might get suspicious. To turn around and run did not seem like a good idea either. Then I remembered Mother skipping across the kitchen. Clutching the package, I began to skip by, hoping that they would pay as little attention to me as

the other German soldiers had. Skip, hop. Skip, hop. The
whole yard was filled with soldiers. Some of the ones on
the street did turn to look at me.

"*Hüpfe, hüpfe*," said one of them, clapping his hands
in rhythm with my movements. I skipped past Mrs.
Silverman's gate, and when I was certain that the soldiers
could no longer see me, I broke into a run.

When I reached home, I had to knock on the gate to be
let in. Mother opened it, her eyes dark green with fear,
and I decided not to tell her about Dr. Feher.

"Mrs. Gerber sent you these," I said in a rush, handing
her the package.

She took it and bolted the gate. Once inside, she un-
rolled the brown paper to find the graceful, tapering green
and gold candles from Mrs. Gerber's mantel. "Now her
house will be empty," Mother said to us as she shook her
head in appreciation of the gift.

Our seder behind locked doors and drawn shades consisted of vegetable soup, potato pancakes, and a lekvár
pudding made from crushed matzos. No prayer books, no
traditional seder plate, no wine. Mother had covered the
table with a white cloth, and Mrs. Gerber's green and gold
candles stood in our brass candleholders at the center as a
festive decoration. Mother lit the candles. The four of
us—Iboya and I, Sandor and Joli—sat down around the
table, and then Mother sat herself in Father's chair and
handed each of us a matzo.

"You children know that tonight is the first night of
seder," she said. "A lot has happened since last Passover,
but we must be grateful that the five of us are here together
tonight. It is traditional in the Passover recital to say,
'Next year in Jerusalem,' but instead, I will say that next
year I want us all to be together with the rest of the family
in Komjaty like we used to be."

Iboya said, "Amen." The rest of us repeated it after
her. Mother got up to serve the soup.

18

Early the next morning, Mr. Hirsch knocked at our door. Mother went out into the yard to talk with him. Iboya and I, watching from the porch, saw Mother cup her face in the palms of her hands, and for a while her body shook with sobs. Then Mr. Hirsch touched her gently on the arm and left.

"I cannot believe it," Mother said slowly. "Dr. Feher shot himself. They have just gotten permission from the Germans to bury him. No funeral—we cannot get into the synagogue and they won't let the rabbi out. But we have to bury him, and I have to be at the cemetery in an hour."

Mother came out of the bedroom dressed in a good dress I had not seen her wear for years, a black silk with a matching jacket, and she held in her hands the hat she used to wear with it. I followed her to the salon. A pale but steady Mother stood in front of the gilded mirror adjusting the hat. "I lost my last good friend who could have helped me," she told the looking glass. I noticed the yellow Star of David pinned to the lapel of her jacket.

"You are going dressed like that?" I asked in surprise. "Isn't it dangerous? I thought you were going to dress in one of your disguises."

"Mr. Hirsch said that it will be all right. The Germans are busy now with reorganizing the government, and the soldiers had their chance the other night." She stopped, sighed, and went on. "And they have the old men locked in the synagogue to amuse them for now. So it should be all right—at least for a while—for us to be out on the street as long as we don't go over the curfew time."

Then she left, and I watched her as she opened the gate and walked up the street in her silk dress and good shoes. For some reason that I didn't understand, tears welled in my eyes.

Mother returned two hours later with the Gerbers. They seemed changed. Even Judi was subdued.

Mrs. Gerber and Mother sat down at the kitchen table and Mrs. Gerber began to tell Mother the contents of a letter she had received from a friend in Budapest. "Hitler's deputy Adolf Eichmann himself came with his SS officers to enforce the new anti-Jewish laws. He gathered up the Jewish community leaders to confer with them and help him carry out the new orders. They are also forcing the Jews entirely out of all professions. The same thing is happening here. That, too, might have had something to do with your Dr. Feher's decision to kill himself."

"No," I interrupted, "I heard someone say that he shot himself because his wife and daughter were . . ."

"Raped," offered Judi boldly.

Mrs. Gerber bowed her head in helplessness. "What will happen to those poor old men in the synagogue? If we don't reach twenty thousand pengö by seven o'clock tonight, they will execute them. We are still short eight thousand and the Germans said they won't extend the time."

"I heard that many Gentiles gave," Mother said.

"I am sure your Mr. Kovacs wasn't one of them. Does he know that you are without money?"

"I am not going back there any more," Mother said, pausing a moment before she continued. "Mr. Hirsch said that they were allowed to take food in to the old men. Some were sick from fright and fatigue. We could have used Dr. Feher in there. In a way, he had no right to take his life. He could have helped while we are still here."

"Did Mr. Hirsch have any idea of what is going to happen to us?"

"He said he'll have more information by next week." Mother looked over to Judi and me. "Why don't the two of you get some plates and set the table on the porch?" Mother said.

"Come on," said Judi, "they want to get rid of us."

Later that afternoon, past curfew time, Mr. Hirsch returned, deeply disturbed. He told Mother that the Germans were getting ready to line up the men in the synagogue and shoot them. "They think we are holding out," he said. "They won't accept the fact that we have no money."

"Where should we have money from?" Mother asked. "They've taken away our incomes and left us nothing."

"We are holding an auction as a last resort. You would not believe what can be bought for five pengö. It is an ugly sight, but we are desperate. The families of the imprisoned men are crying and pleading with us to save their fathers and grandfathers. And if we let it happen to them this time, who will be next?"

Mother moved around the kitchen and picked up the brass candlesticks and the brass mortar and pestle she kept on the shelf of the kitchen cupboard. She handed them to Mr. Hirsch.

"Can I come and help?" asked Iboya.

"We are using only our sons for now. There will be time for you to help with other things," he answered. He thanked Mother for the things she had given him and promised to send us word of the outcome of the sale. Then he was gone.

We heard nothing further that night. I lay awake in bed straining to hear the sound of gunfire from Main Street and yet terrified of hearing it. Hearing nothing, though, but the breathing of the others in the room, I finally fell asleep. The next morning, Mr. Schwartz stopped by on the way to his fish store to tell Mother that the men had been let out at ten o'clock the night before.

The same day, Mr. Hirsch came to tell Mother the deportation orders. Eichmann had divided Hungary into six zones, and the first to be evacuated would be our area and the surrounding villages. My mind leaped to thoughts of Babi and Rozsi, and I didn't hear anything else that he said. After he left, we did our chores and ate our sparse meal. A word from any one of us and we would have started to cry. It was enough just to be close to one another.

Early the following morning, we were awakened by strange sounds of movement in our street. We came out onto the porch in our nightshirts to see our street lined with slowly moving wagons and walking refugees—mostly women. We went back inside and quickly dressed ourselves and the children. Mother told Sandor to keep Joli inside while she, Iboya, and I went down to the gate and watched as the carts and wagons, pulled mostly by oxen, with an old horse appearing occasionally, crawled by. In the wagons, heaped high with bundles, rode the infants, the old, and the sick. Hungarian policemen and German soldiers with bayonets fixed to their rifles walked alongside the wagons. After watching this procession in uncomprehending silence for about fifteen minutes, Mother stopped one of the Hungarian policemen and asked, very politely, where all of these people were from and where they were being taken.

"Jews from the villages outside of Beregszász," he said scornfully. "They are being taken to the brick factory, now the ghetto."

"What is a ghetto?" I asked Mother as soon as the policeman had gone back to his place in the line of march.

She answered my question in a firm tone of voice, "It is a place for people who have been separated from the rest of the community."

I turned away to look again at the people in the road. Some of the women walking behind the wagons were crying. One of them looked at us and spoke: "Dear ladies, some water please for my feverish son." Another one asked for a diaper for her baby. A third wanted some bread for her father. "Gracious ladies . . ." The pleading continued without stop. I could not look into their faces. They represented something terrifying. Their bodies walked, their mouths spoke words, but their eyes were vacant and hopeless.

Mother told me to draw water from the well and to give it to those people I could reach. She took Iboya back into the house with her, and after a while Iboya returned to pass out diapers torn from sheets. I carried the buckets of water, handing cupfuls to the old and sick. I tried to run up to the wagons with the Hungarian police guards, rather than the ones the German soldiers were walking beside, but except for an occasional shove or grunt, the German soldiers let me be. People handed me whatever utensils they had to be filled with water from the bucket. "Pretty miss, dear young lady, God should bless you, a blessing on your head," I kept hearing as I continued to empty out our well, taking only short rests until dusk, when Mother called us to come inside. But the procession continued, even while we slept.

By the third day there was a big drop in the water mark inside the cement pipe of the well. My hands, chafed from cranking and pulling on the iron chain, were wrapped in rags. Mother, not having anything left to give, stayed in the house with Sandor and Joli. She came out to check on me and pull up a bucket of water at regular intervals.

The next day, Iboya and some of her friends borrowed Mr. Schwartz's wagon and his horse, who was too old to be confiscated, and went from one Jewish house to another, collecting anything that could be of help to the people in the ghetto. A number of them had been forced to leave without a change of clothing, without bedding and blankets, and in some cases without the medication they needed on a regular basis. She came home at dusk exhausted after several trips to the ghetto.

"Iboya, what is it like? Where do the people sleep?" I asked her on the fifth morning of the march to the ghetto as she was preparing to leave for her day of collecting.

"We are only allowed to the gate," she answered. "The white arm band simply means that I belong to the youth service group of the Juden Bureau and don't have to obey the curfew. I don't know what it is like inside."

After Iboya had gone, Mother turned her flour sack upside down to bake the last of the flour into bread. "I am not going to bother to save the growing yeast for the next baking," she said. "There is no next. This is the last of our flour, and who will be here to bake bread?"

I had once asked Mother about the neat little ball of dough she always saved from her Friday baking and tucked inside a flowered tin box for the following Friday. She had answered, "I brought this tin box with me from Komjaty when I first moved to Beregszász. My mother gave me a ball of her growing yeast to take with me. She got her original ball of dough from her mother. This way the bread we bake stays the same for generations.''

"Are you going to give me a ball of the dough when I get married?" I asked.

"Of course," she had answered.

I stood now remembering that promise and watching her scrape up every morsel of dough from her wooden kneading bowl. With a determined expression on her face, she formed it into the last loaf of bread. Over the next few evenings I watched her sitting at the stove, the top plate covered with even slices of bread. She sat and patiently turned the slices until they were browned on both sides. Satisfied that they were done, she placed them in a pillow case.

"Why are you making all the bread into toast?" I asked.

"Bread mildews, but toast keeps," she replied.

Mother kept reminding me each day as I ran out to fill the first bucket with water, "Piri, don't forget to ask if any of them have come from around Komjaty. And if someone has, come and get me right away." I knew that she was anxious for news of Babi and Rozsi.

One day during this time, I ran after a wagon with a very sick old lady lying on the top, propped up by bundles, to hand her a cup of water. Her hands shook as she reached for it, and I climbed up on the side of the wagon to hold her hand against the cup so that the water would not spill out. Her hand felt smooth, warm, and leathery dry, like Babi's. I let the wagon carry me for a short distance, holding on to her hand until one of the guards made me jump off. I walked back to my bucket on the sidewalk feeling very depressed. I let my mind wander for the first time since the procession had started. "Where is my Babi?" I wondered. The answer came the next day in a letter from Molcha. No return address, I noticed right away, but I recognized her simple and round lettering.

The letter was dated April 26, 1944. It had taken only four days to reach me. The first sentence answered my question: "We are the first to arrive in the Szölös ghetto. They have not yet emptied the city. I'm giving this letter to one of our ghetto police. He promised to pass it over the fence." I read on quickly. German soldiers had come along with the Hungarian police to take them from their homes. They were given thirty minutes to get out, and allowed one bundle each. Molcha's father insisted on taking his tinker's tools. They did not stop him. When Molcha's family got out to the oxcart at Babi's gate, they overheard one of the Hungarian policemen tell the two German soldiers that Babi refused to leave. Molcha and her mother went in to see if they could help avoid an incident. Babi was sitting in her chair holding her prayer book. Rozsi was crying in her helplessness. Molcha's mother told Babi, "You will get us all in trouble with your stubborn ways," as she helped Rozsi lift her out of her chair and carry her to the waiting oxcart.

In her last sentence, Molcha asked, "No matter what happens, can we remain friends forever?" I finished the letter, and then with great reluctance handed it to Mother. Her eyes filled with tears as she read it. She let the tears spill down her white cheeks. "My mother left her land after all," she said in a husky voice. "What an end to have lived for! Abiding with God every step of the way, too. Where is justice, O God? And my poor Rozsi." Mother sat down and, spreading out writing paper, composed a desperate scheme to try to save Babi from further harm. She addressed the letter to our relatives in Szölös and asked me to post it directly.

We never knew what happened to that letter, but the next day we did get a letter from Rozsi, the last we ever received, telling us that they were all right and that Babi, still as strong and firm in belief as ever, was helping to keep everyone calm. Maybe we will all be sent to the same place in Germany, Rozsi concluded, saying that she was looking forward to being reunited with us.

Finally on Friday, after seven days of constant movement, the street was empty of refugees. My water bucket was no longer needed and I could see the road again. The quiet made Mother jumpy. She kept looking for an explanation. She waited for the mailman, sent me to the corner to buy a newspaper, and looked up and down both sides of the street.

"I have lived on this street for over twenty years, but I have never seen it so deserted for this length of time. No one has ever come over to say one word to me in the seven days since the procession started," she said.

As I walked back with the newspaper, I noticed that the buds on the chestnut trees lining both sidewalks had opened and the small, fragile shiny leaves were uncurling under the sunny sky. Back in our yard, Sandor and Joli, permitted again to leave the house, were back to their never-ending make-believe in the sandbox, with the large walnut tree shading them like an open umbrella. Mother was standing watching them. Taking the paper from me, she sat down in Lilli's chair. It had become a permanent part of the yard. Nobody had moved it since the day Lilli left. The light spring breeze carried the scent of the walnut leaves and mixed it with all the other earthy smells of growth. My head was slightly dazed by spring fever, yet Mother's sudden idleness made me very uneasy.

THE GHETTO

THE GHETTO

19

The next morning I awoke with the same feeling of uneasiness and heard Mother arguing with Iboya.

"You are not going on the wagon today. I want you to stay home with us. Besides, it is the Sabbath."

"I rode on the wagon all over the city last Saturday and you didn't stop me," Iboya protested.

"Today I want you to stay home," Mother replied.

"I can't. I promised to meet the others on Main Street, and they will be waiting for me. We have to collect as much food, bedding, and clothing as we can. Time is running out." With these last words, Iboya was out the door.

Later I went into the yard to hand my phonograph over the back fence to Ica Molnar.

"Keep it for me, just in case we have to go away," I told her. "You can play my records. I'll go and get them." I turned from Ica's stunned face. We had not seen much of each other since I had been forbidden to attend public school with her. When we met on the street, we didn't seem to have anything to say. She was still Ica Molnar, but I had lost my old identity of her equal. I had been classified as an undesirable citizen—a Jew—and Ica had learned to keep her distance from me. Now, confronted by my entrusting her with my most valued possession, Ica was at a loss for words. Her helplessness came through in her pale blue eyes. "I did not mean to cause you harm," they pleaded as she accepted the weight of the heavy machine. I turned away faster than I had to. It hurt me to see her distressed.

I had just started back to the vegetable garden when Mother's voice pierced my ears. "Piri, Piri, where are you?"

Running past the woodshed, I turned toward the porch and saw that our yard had been invaded. Military and police uniforms mingled. Strange male voices spoke, asked question, and gave orders. Surrounded by hostile men, Mother stood holding Joli in her arms and Sandor by the hand. I felt an anger rise inside me and wished that I were able to protect my mother and the two little ones. One of the men stood reading the names the census taker had posted on our porch.

"Where is Etu?" he asked.

"She does not live at home. She is away at school."

The Hungarian policeman took out a notebook. "Her address?"

Mother hesitated. "I have not heard from her in a long time."

"What was her address when she last wrote?"

"I'll go and look for her letter."

"Wait. Next is Iboya. Where is she?"

"Go look for her," Mother cried to me.

I hated leaving them, the two children clinging for comfort, and Mother herself so shaken. The policeman closest to me shoved me into motion. "Do as you're told," he growled. "And don't take all day."

I left our crowded yard and ran, tearing through our street toward Main Street. I ran past our shoe store and suddenly wished I had a pair of new shoes. I looked into the fur shop next door and thought of Lujza, mangled dead by a train. I ran past Dr. Feher's office and remembered him in his white coat. He, too, was dead. Dead, I repeated to myself as I ran past the temple yard. Seeing the German tanks there, I remembered that I had forgotten to wear my yellow star. But no one stopped me for questioning. The temple doors were open. German uniforms milled around, throaty German sounds carried out to the street. I hurried on in search of the open wagon harnessed to Mr. Schwartz's old horse, but there was no trace of the wagon, Iboya, or Iboya's friends. I looked into the café where Lujza had once bought me a pastry. The faces and voices inside had changed. Uniforms and sounds of German laughter crowded the open room. I was out of breath and wet with perspiration. Where was I to look?

Growing more anxious and aware of the passing time, I bumped into a man carrying a briefcase as I ran around a corner. He looked annoyed, but just rushed past me. Stopping to lean against the wall of a house to catch my breath, I remembered Mother and the children as I had left them, surrounded by those strangers in uniform. I started to cry out of helplessness and resumed my running, tasting salty tears in the corners of my mouth. I was not at all sure that I had taken the right course, or that I was searching the right streets. Finally, just as I passed the cobbler's shop, I spotted the wagon with the lone horse.

A friend of Iboya's sat on the box smoking a cigarette. Behind him, an assortment of bundles lay strewn in disarray.

"Where is my sister Iboya?" I asked him.

"Inside. I'll go get her." He looked me over with questioning eyes, threw the cigarette butt into the gutter, and went into the building.

When I saw Iboya come through the gate, I let go of all restraint. "They've come to take us away. You have to come home right away!"

"We'll take you," said her friend, lighting another cigarette.

"No need." Iboya shook her head. "Continue on."

Several other boys and girls came through the gate carrying bundles. "We'll be joining you shortly," they called after us.

Iboya looked cross as she examined my face. "Why are you crying? You'll just give yourself a headache."

"Mother looked scared when they asked her questions, and I had to come to look for you. What if they take her away and don't wait for us?" I blurted out.

"We know where to find them." Iobya started running, and I fell into step behind her. It took all of my energy to keep up with her as the strong noonday sun beat over our heads. When we reached Gyar Street, a wagon stood outside our gate facing in the direction of the brick factory. A driver sat on the box with his back toward us. As we came through the gate, we could see Mother sitting on one of the porch benches with Joli on her lap and Sandor sitting next to her. She jumped up when she saw us. We stepped up on the porch to see uniformed men walking through the rooms of the house, looking at and touching everything.

The Hungarian policeman with the notebook came out onto the porch. "Iboya," he said, and crossed her name off the census list posted on the porch wall. "Piri." He put a black line through my name. "Mrs. Ignac Davidowitz, Sandor, Joli"—a black line was run through each name as he pronounced it. He had written Etu's name and address in his notebook.

Iboya walked away from us, went into the summer kitchen, and came out carrying a heavy duffel bag. The policeman who had shoved me stepped up to her. "Untie the string and empty the bag," he said. Mother and I looked in amazement at the contents she scattered on the porch floor at his command—a box of notepaper, pencils, some intimate feminine articles, a large box of aspirin tablets, and several books. Iboya's face flushed as the policeman kicked at the articles with his boot and looked into some of the books he picked up. "You may gather it up," he said, and kicked again at the bolt of absorbent cotton and the crocheted sanitary napkins.

"Let's go," said the policeman.

I realized that I had not packed anything to take with me, but I could not go into the house with all of them walking through. Iboya finished putting her things back in the bag. Mother held up the key to the front door, indicating that she would like to lock up.

"No need for that. The doors and windows will be bolted," the policeman said crossly.

Mother dropped the key back into her purse, put Joli down, stood up, and picked up the pillowcase full of toast and a large suitcase that she had kept packed for the past week. Iboya and I picked up as many of the tied bundles as we could. Sandor and Joli, as they stepped off the porch, made a dash for the sandbox. Gathering up some of their toys, they ran back, frightened that they might be punished. Mother stopped at the gate and turned to look back, waiting. The German soldiers were coming out of the house.

"*Gehen Sie!*" said one of them as he reached us at the gate.

"*Ich will mein Türe schliessen, bitte.*" Mother made another attempt to lock up.

"*Gehen Sie!*" he repeated, poking her back with the end of his club. Mother shrugged and boarded the wagon. Iboya handed up the children with their toys. I was next. Iboya gathered up the remainder of our bundles and, after handing them to me, came up with her duffel bag. Mother was looking back at the soldiers.

"Take a good look, woman," said the policeman with the sarcastic voice. "I doubt you'll ever see it again." He motioned the driver to move on while he walked alongside. Mother rode backwards, sitting on top of the bundles. Sandor and Joli were staying very close to her. I noticed Ica and her mother looking out from behind their curtains as the wagon moved past their house. I looked at Mother; her face seemed old and tired, her green eyes sunk deep and black. I couldn't think of anything to say, so I just turned away from her and looked straight ahead.

I had walked this road many times, and it seemed odd to be making the same trip on top of a wagon. The horse walked at a very slow pace, and the driver never even turned to look at us. After Gyár Street, there were no more houses; the road opened up to the park on the right and the lumber yard on the left.

As we passed it, I remembered falling into the pond at the edge of the park years before. I had been wearing a white piqué dress at the time. Lured by the sight of some delicate blue flowers at the rim of the pond, I had, in reaching out and pulling them from the moist earth by their roots, lost my balance. I slid into the pond, white dress, patent leather shoes, and all. I climbed out and saw that my dress was covered with green slime, and my shoes sloshed with muddy water. When I got home, Mother had to leave the company she was entertaining to clean me up, and she was angry.

From my perch in the wagon I could see the same blue

forget-me-nots blooming. No one else noticed them. Mother and Iboya sat grim and silent, each with her own thoughts. The brick factory came into view. A wooden gate had been built in front of it, and there were soldiers patrolling in front of the gate, as well as around the open fields that surrounded the factory. One of them recognized Iboya, as we drew close, from the many trips she had made there.

"So it is your turn now, is it?" he said to her.

Iboya nodded and tried to look brave. The wagon stopped, and we got off. When the driver threw our bundles on the dusty road, I saw his face for the first time. It was old, deeply lined, and his eyes, which I glanced into for a moment, showed no emotion. He looked tired and bored.

Two young men with white arm bands met us on the other side of the gate and helped us with the parcels. The younger of the two smiled at me as he bent to pick up a bundle.

"You'll be staying in number 6," he said.

We followed the two men, carrying the rest of our sacks and looking at the faces of the women and few men we passed. They all looked back in sympathetic kinship. Some women even offered to help us carry our bundles.

We entered one of the sheds of the brickworks, but this was not the brick factory I remembered. The busy workers had been replaced by crowds of idle families. There was no singing here, only a low-pitched din of voices. Gone were the bricks and the cars used to transport them. Nothing but bundles and people crowded this shed, which had no walls, only a clay-tiled roof held up by wooden pillars. People either sat on their bundles or stood around in clusters. Some of the elderly were propped up, lying on the earth floor of the shed.

The two young men came to an empty spot on the left side of shed number 6 and dropped our bundles on the ground.

"This area between these two posts will be your home. You'll have to confine yourselves within its boundaries. We are running out of space," the older of the two said. They turned and walked away, leaving us standing there in the area, which was two and a half by three meters.

Mother sat down on the valise and looked about at her new surroundings. A woman, holding the hand of a little girl about Joli's age, wandered toward us across the narrow iron car tracks. She was younger than Mother and in a disheveled state.

"My name is Mrs. Labovitz and this is my daughter Carla. Maybe our children can play together while we are neighbors," she said. "I am without my family. Just the two of us. We got separated from my mother and my sisters. I can't find out anything about them." The little girl reached for Joli's pail.

"Where are you from?" Mother asked the woman.

"Tolcsva. We were on our way to visit my in-laws when they picked me and the child up on the road."

Mother and I looked over the tracks to their space to see a lone open suitcase.

Following our glance with her eyes, the woman said, "That is all we have. Where are you coming from?"

Mother stood up to point in the direction of our house. "If the road did not curve, you could see my house. It is just at the end of the road, where it runs into Gyár Street. The street got its name from this factory." Mother stood motionless, facing in the direction of our street, and when she turned back and lowered her hand, I noticed a film of moisture bathing her eyes.

"Oh," said the woman, "you are city people. I could tell right away . . . You brought some of your bedding and all."

"Pardon me," Iboya interrupted. "I might be able to get you some blankets. My friends will be coming to the gate around five o'clock. I'll see if I can go and meet them."

"You will have a mitzvah," the woman blessed her. "We sat up all last night—my little Carla and I. The ground is so cold and hard."

After she once again looked all around us, Mother's face registered a decision. "We will all have to get busy and do something instead of just standing about." Untying the biggest bundle, she took out her two bedspreads and, turning to Iboya and me, said, "Please give me a hand. I am going to hang these up for some privacy." With a few nails she dug out of her purse, and a rock for a hammer, she hung one of the bedspreads from the wood beams of the outside rafter, separating us from the crowd in the shed immediately next to us.

"You girls go find us some bricks, and we can build ourselves a table and some seats. Is there water anywhere?" She addressed this question to the onlookers who had gathered around us. "We can't just sit and let ourselves grow dirty. We have to try and help ourselves. We must not let them think that we are a dirty lot." By this time, Mother had gathered quite an audience.

Some agreed with trying to get organized. Others smirked. "What good would it do to settle in? Even if we could manage it, we'll only be here for a few days. We might even be transported tomorrow."

"Then," Mother answered, "let us do it for today. It is still better than just standing around."

The few elderly men in the crowd started to talk among themselves. "She does have a point. It will give us something to do."

A boy about my age said, "I saw a shallow pond at the end of the shed."

Mother unpacked a pot from the opened bundle and gave it to him. "See if you can get some water, so that the mothers can wash their children."

The boy stood still, too scared to move. "I might get in trouble with the guards," he said. "They watch every move we make."

Some people in the crowd agreed with him. "Sure, she is going to get us all in trouble."

"Is there anyone in charge here?" Mother asked.

A man came forward. "My name is Shuster, and I'm in charge." A white band encircled his right arm. He pushed through the people surrounding Mother and stood confronting her. "They are right," he said with authority. "We are not to roam. They want everyone in his assigned place at all times."

A woman came out of the crowd and tugged at the boy's shoulder. He placed the pot Mother had given him on the ground; the woman took him by the hand, and they walked away.

The crowd dispersed as Mother silently returned to her unpacking. She managed to make us a place to sit and an area to unroll our bedding. She put her pots and utensils into a pillowcase and hid the pillowcase filled with toast under a blanket. She got the little ones busy with their toys in a corner of the space against the hanging bedspread.

Then she came over to Iboya and me where we sat on the suitcase watching her. "Tomorrow," she said, "we will have to look around for the Gerbers. If the Germans started with our side of town, they won't get to the Gerbers until tomorrow. Maybe we could have them stay near us. Iboya, you try to meet your friends at five o'clock. Piri will go with you and talk to the young man who showed us to this spot. He liked you," she said to me with a smile, "and you might pick up some information. It will not do for us to sit here and be frightened like the rest."

Mr. Shuster reappeared and looked around, much impressed with the order he saw. "I have to post your names," he said, passing me a pencil and piece of paper. I wrote down our names, he took a nail from his pocket, and as I held the paper in place, he hammered the list up on the supporting beam nearest us.

"Could I have a few of your nails?" Mother asked him. "I just brought a couple, and I've already used them."

He dug into his pocket again, brought out four nails, and handed them to Mother. "I am sorry for not having been able to support you in your enthusiasm to get organized," he said, "but I was given strict orders to keep the people in this shed quiet and in their places. They are allowed to go only to the latrine, and they must come right back."

"I am surprised that you would accept such orders," Mother said firmly. "These are people, not cattle. If they can't do anything for themselves but stand around to debate their uncertain fate and move only to go to the latrine, they will soon turn into just what the Germans want to believe we are—dirty vermin. Look around you at some of these poor women. They've started to let themselves go already.''

''We have only been here two days,'' Mr. Shuster replied. ''I have spoken to people who have been here longer, and they say that some of them have privileges during certain hours. I thought I might talk to the German inspectors when they come by on their tour today.''

''My daughter Iboya has been working with the youth service group on the outside ever since this factory became a ghetto. You will have to let her go to the gate and meet her friends at five o'clock. Maybe she could bring some blankets for that poor unfortunate woman across the way.'' She pointed to Mrs. Labovitz and Carla as she spoke. Mr. Shuster tied to interrupt, but Mother continued, ''Mr. Shuster, if we allow them to make us so afraid of them, we are giving them the power to be our superiors.''

Mr. Shuster shook his head. ''I can't take the responsibility.''

''You don't have to see her go.''

''Mrs. Davidowitz, I admire your courage. Wherever she may be, I hope my wife has half as much as you do. But you must remember that I am responsible for the safety of all of these people.'' Sweeping his right arm around in a circle to indicate the entire shed, he turned and walked away, leaving some curious eyes and stretched necks wondering what he and Mother had been talking about.

Mother made Iboya and me tidy our hair and gave us each a fresh blouse from the suitcase. ''Pretend that you are one of the inside group of helpers and act confident,'' she said to Iboya.

''What about me?'' I asked.

''You can walk her part of the way and then wait and watch for her.''

We left by the back entrance to the shed, the way people went to use the latrine, so that we would not have to pass Mr. Shuster. We walked up to shed number 1 and waited there until Iboya spotted the white-arm-banded group of inside helpers walking to the gate. She hurried over and fell into step with them. I saw them stop, hesitate for a moment, then continue on in the direction of the gate. From where I stood, I could see the latrine. I wondered why they had to dig the long ditch so near the road in full view of the guards and of any passers-by. How embarrassing to sit on that log knowing that all those people could see you. I knew that I would wait until dark before I used it.

I watched as Iboya and the others came back from the gate with the bundles. I ran to catch up with them.

"We have to take these things straight to the supply house," Iboya said. "The people in charge there decide who will get these supplies." I helped Iboya to carry some of her load.

The young man who had shown us to our shed when we arrived smiled at me again. "Maybe you can sign up with your sister and join our group," he said as he started to walk alongside of us.

"But she is only . . ." Iboya had begun to say "thirteen," but I quickly cut in before she could finish and said, "Fourteen." I could feel my face flush from lying; my birthday was nearly two months away.

"My name is Henri," said the young man. "What is yours?"

"Piri," I answered shyly and we continued to walk in silence. In the shed where the supplies were stored, articles of clothing and bedding filled the shelves. One of the Hungarian policemen came to take the bundles from us.

"I would like to ask for one of the pillows and two blankets for a mother and child in shed number 6," Iboya said in a polite but firm tone.

"We decide who gets what," he answered curtly.

"But they don't have anything with them. They have to sleep uncovered on the bare ground."

"The man in charge of her shed has to hand in a requisition."

We started to turn away when one of the young men in the group spoke up. "What she did not tell you, Mr. Toron, is that this woman is sick and we have no room for her in the infirmary. They have just arrived."

The policeman turned to a shelf and took down a ragged

blanket. "She can have this one for now," he said, handing it to Iboya, "but for anything else you will have to get a requisition from the man in charge of your shed."

Iboya nodded and we all left. Once we were outside, Iboya asked the young man who had spoken up why they kept all those supplies in there instead of giving them to the people who needed them.

"First they go through everything and take the best things for themselves; then they stall with the rest," he answered.

"I would not have worked so hard to get the things had I known," Iboya said angrily.

"There is a lot you two don't know yet."

"I would like to ask a few questions," I said. "For one, is that the only toilet?" I pointed to the latrine.

"No, there is one in the rear, but your group has to use the front one."

"We can't. It's too degrading."

"Then you will have to sneak down there."

"And what about food?"

"There is bread for breakfast with some kind of hot drink they call tea. And the soup should be coming right about now."

"They don't overfeed us."

"They are holding out on everything."

"When is the curfew?"

"Before nine in the morning and after seven in the evening, and you can walk only in certain designated areas. You are out of your area now."

Then Henri joined in the conversation. "I should be taking you back right now. I am one of the police for your area."

"Not until we use the latrine in the back," Iboya said.

"Hurry up. It is in back of number 12. Then I will walk you back."

The other five members of the inside group said, "*Szervusz*" and walked away.

Iboya and I found the back latrine; it was not much better than the front one. Although there were walls, it was open at both ends. Again there was the same narrow ditch with boards over it propped to form a long bench into which numerous holes had been cut. As much as we disliked it, we had to use it. I wished that Henri was not waiting for us. I did not want to see him just then, it was all too humiliating. But he was there when we emerged, and to hide my embarrassment, I asked, "What is it like to live in the ghetto?" He hesitated. "You have to learn to not mind being hungry, cold, or wet, and don't get sick—there's no medicine. They'll beat you if you disobey, and kill you if you try to escape." When we got back to our place in the shed, Mother confronted him with more questions.

"What if it rains during the night?" she asked. "We'll all get soaked. Why won't they let us build walls for some privacy and shelter?"

"They are not planning to keep us here very long," Henri answered. "Just until they get some trains."

"Where are they taking us?"

"To Germany. That's all any of us know."

Mother thanked him for everything and asked him to stop by again. I walked with him to the end of the shed.

"I have seen you before," he said. I was shocked. "You were carrying a water bucket. You climbed on the wagon that carried my grandmother and held the drinking cup for her."

"You passed through our street? I don't remember seeing you."

"No, you were very busy."

"How is your grandmother?"

"She is in the infirmary. Would you like to come with me to see her tomorrow? I'll come by for you."

"Yes," I said, "I'd like that."

"*Szervusz.*"

"*Szervusz.*"

Henri walked on, and I returned to our place inside the shed where Iboya was telling Mother what we had learned from our walk with the inside group of youth workers. Supper came, served from a food wagon by harassed women on kitchen detail, supervised by German guards. The turnip soup was watery, and the bread stale, but nobody complained. They begged for more. Mother put all of our portions into her big pot and added some seasoning from her jars. She invited Mrs. Labovitz and Carla to join us, and she put a pinch of seasoning in their bowls, too. After we finished our soup, Mr. Shuster came by, smoking his pipe.

"I'd like to talk with you," Mother said to him.

"What about?"

"About your list. I understand that you are to write up a list of our complaints."

"I am new at this game, Mrs. Davidowitz; be patient. By now you probably know more about this place than I do."

"But you are in charge. I am not trying to be difficult, but we should claim some rights. We can't have them think we are sitting cows."

"Tomorrow we can visit in the other quarters. I have posted the time and limits at the front."

"The list of things we need, Mr. Shuster. My girls saw the supplies. They have plenty of everything, but you must submit a list." Mother ran across to Mrs. Labovitz's place and held up the torn blanket. "This is what they gave this poor woman and child."

Mother's demonstration caused a commotion. All the people around wanted to know where the blanket had come from. And now they all wanted different things. About fifty people crowded around us. It took all of Mr. Shuster's ability to get them quieted down and back to their places.

While Mr. Shuster was dealing with the people who had crowded about, Mother made some more walls, hanging the other bedspread and a sheet over the rafters. Then she took one of Iboya's notebooks from the duffel bag, tore out a page, found a pencil, and sat down on the suitcase to make a list. Water was first, latrine walls second.

Mr. Shuster ducked into our tent-like cubicle and looked over Mother's shoulder. "Mind putting down 'pipe tobacco'?" he asked in a kidding voice, hoarse from his shouting.

"I'm really sorry about what happened. I didn't mean to cause a riot," whispered Mother, "but unless we do something, we are all going to get sick. We can't live in these crowded conditions without some sanitary precautions. We have to get this point across to them. Scare them, if necessary; tell them that if an epidemic of typhus breaks out, it will spread to the city. They have made no provisions at all, just shipping people in here like cattle. But even cattle need water."

"Mrs. Davidowitz, they have no intention of keeping us here. They are merely waiting for trains."

"But some of these people have been here over a week already. They are starting to smell."

"Get some of these women to stop letting the children use the ground between the sheds instead of taking them to the assigned latrines. When the Germans see what is happening, they say that we are swine and don't need water."

"The children are afraid to sit on those logs. And what happens during the night? Are we allowed out there at all after seven?"

"Not after the curfew."

"So there is your answer. They give us no choice."

"Make the list," said Mr. Shuster with a resigned sigh. "I'll see if they will consider any of our grievances."

When he had left with the list, I felt very tired and asked Mother if I could go to sleep. As she rolled out the bedding, she decided that we all should try to get some sleep. Closing my eyes at the end of this first day in the ghetto, I told myself that the five of us were still together and that was the most important thing.

20

The next day was Sunday, and the rest of the Jewish population of Beregszász started to pour into the brick factory in a steady stream. Iboya, now a member of the ghetto work force, watched for the Gerbers. Mother had managed to talk Mr. Shuster into letting her stake out an area alongside of ours to accommodate them. While we waited for the Gerbers to appear, we watched the new arrivals as they came in. Mother ran from family to family, helping them settle their bundles and soothing the old and the children. Sandor and Joli remained in their corner, digging in the dirt floor, thinking up new games.

I wandered off and, keeping within the allowed limits, moved from shed to shed, asking some of the people I saw where they had come from and how long they had been in the ghetto. I was hoping to hear something more about Babi, Rozsi, and Molcha. A number of them recognized me as the girl with the water bucket, but none of them had any news for me.

For a while I stood outside the sheds and watched the groups of people coming through the gates. Had we looked like that yesterday when we arrived? Was I as frightened, I wondered. They walked close to each other, their eyes looking about as though they expected a wolf or a tiger to leap at them any moment. Hardly any men among them— they were mostly clusters of women and children, the mothers invariably carrying a child. Many old women needed support as they were being walked down the road through swirls of red clay dust.

Then I saw Gari Weiss, wearing the white arm band of the ghetto police, escorting a group of new arrivals. He looked very self-important as he pointed to a shed several yards in front of them. I felt none of the apprehension that I had felt at school when I wanted so much to speak to him and didn't dare. When he returned from the shed he had pointed out, I went up to him and started talking, amazed at my ease in conversing with him. A few other youth police joined us, and Gari introduced me to them as his schoolmate from B.G. I was puzzled and asked what he meant. "Before ghetto," he explained. We all laughed at the joke, and the others walked on.

"Is Judi here yet?" Gari asked, coloring slightly.

"No. As a matter of fact, I would like you to do me a big favor. If you should see the Gerbers coming in, please bring them to our shed, number 6, because my mother is saving a place for them."

"I have heard about your mother," said Gari.

"What have you heard?"

"That she has set up a tent inside your shed."

"So what if she has? It does not protect us from the night's cold winds. She just wanted to make us some privacy."

"Hey, I wasn't criticizing. I just said I heard about it."

"Where are you and your family staying? Are you still in the big house in back of the factory just as you were B.G.?"

"Not exactly," Gari answered. "The German guards now have our house. We are living in the maids' house behind it."

"I'm sorry."

"No, don't be, we are still better off than the rest of you."

Henri and his friends came walking toward us on their way back to the gate after settling some families. As he went by, he said, *"Szervusz,"* and I stopped the group to ask Henri if I could walk with him to the gate.

"I am waiting for a friend to arrive," I explained.

Gari smirked knowingly and turned away, walking back to the gate by himself to pick up a new group of arrivals.

I was annoyed at Gari's manner, but I fell into step with Henri and his friends.

"I don't know if we will get a chance to visit my grandmother before curfew this evening," Henri said. "It seems that they have decided to empty the rest of Beregszász today."

"Do you know Gari?" I asked.

"Sure. We've been working together. He may seem conceited, but he has a good heart."

"Did you talk to him about my mother's tent?"

"Yes. I told him how much I admire her, trying to make you comfortable under these trying conditions. She is a very special lady."

I smiled at him and said, "The family I am looking for are close friends of ours by the name of Gerber. There are three of them, Mrs. Gerber, Judi, who is my friend, and Pali, her younger brother. My mother is saving a place beside us for them."

"Your sister has already alerted all of us on gate duty. One of us should spot them."

I said goodbye to Henri and returned to our shed. The Gerbers arrived about four o'clock that afternoon. Gari saw them come through the gate and brought them to join us. They had walked all the way and were exhausted. The supply of wagons had run out, Mrs. Gerber explained, and the Germans made them walk.

"They threw our things on a wagon," Mrs. Gerber continued. "I hope we'll get them."

Pulling out a few pieces of dry toast from her pillowcase under the blanket, Mother handed a slice to each of the Gerbers. "Eat it inside the tent. No sense in causing another commotion," she said, and went on to relate the incident of the blanket.

Mrs. Gerber ate her piece of toast and looked around at Sandor and Joli's new dirt sandbox, the roll-up beds made of blankets lined with sheets, the large suitcase lying flat as a table, and the remaining bundles around it as chairs. "Rise, you are playing house. I can't believe your ingenuity and your spirit. You are an incorrigible actress. Even here you find yourself a part to play."

"Play? I am just trying not to give in to them. I don't want to become one of the *Schwein*. But we won't go into that now. You are tired. Look at your swollen feet. You must rest. Time enough tomorrow to talk about what is going on."

Iboya had located some of the Gerbers' belongings, and she managed to replace the blankets that were lost or taken from supplies brought in by her friends.

"Did you take these from the supply shed?" Mother asked softly when she brought them into our tent.

"No, I could never get in there. I just did not bother to deliver these to the shed."

"Don't get yourself in any trouble," Mother cautioned.

On the second day after Judi's arrival, we were standing outside our shed observing a work detail answering Mother's demand for water. A youth worker lined up people holding utensils and led them to the water pump. Each filled his pot in turn and then carried the water back to his shed. Another work group, using boards that had come to us from the lumber yard, was hammering up walls for the latrine. Iboya, who now returned to the shed only to sleep, came to us carrying some old clothes. She asked me to hold them for her, dug into the pocket of her skirt, and brought out two aspirins, which she put in her mouth and swallowed.

"How can you swallow them without water?" Judi asked, grimacing.

"You learn to do all kinds of things when you have to," Iboya replied. She lifted the clothes from my arms and started to walk away.

"Where are you going now?" I asked.

"Sorry, I can't talk. See you later." She strode away, disappearing among the groups of people. Then we saw the gate of the ghetto, closed since the last families arrived, open to admit a truckful of gray-uniformed German soldiers armed with rifles coming in for their daily inspection tour of the ghetto. They dismounted from the truck and lined up to begin their inspection. *"Schwein,"* we heard several times as they went from shed to shed.

Judi and I watched the white-arm-banded helpers like Iboya who organized the work details. They took orders from the Germans, but at the same time they tried to get concessions from them to make life in the ghetto more bearable for us. We wished we were old enough to work with them. Tired of watching, Judi and I went back into the shed. Mrs. Gerber and Mother were quietly talking and Judi joined them. But I was still thinking of being part of the work force. Sometimes we heard them singing popular tunes while they hammered or carried food from the kitchen. I dug into Iboya's duffel bag, found her notebook and a pencil, pulled out a page, and wrote some new lyrics to one of the popular melodies I had heard—lyrics more suited to our new life in the ghetto.

Henri appeared just as I finished. He explained that his grandmother, sick in the infirmary, would like to see the girl who had given her water on the way to the ghetto. Mother gave permission for me to go with him. I left the

shed, still holding the piece of notepaper on which I'd
written the new words to the old melody.

"What is that you're holding?" Henri asked as we
walked.

I told him what I had written. He took the sheet from
me, read it, and smiled. "Well, we will have to try these
words," he said with amusement. "You'll be known now
as the ghetto-lyrics girl as well as the water-bucket girl."

The infirmary was a closed barracks with makeshift cots
lining both sides of the long walls. As we reached Henri's
grandmother's cot, she saw us and made an effort to pull
herself up. Her dark brown eyes sparkled in her wrinkled
face.

"So you kept your promise, Henri, and brought me a
visitor," she said softly in Yiddish, sounding a lot like
Babi. "But you did not tell me that the young lady would
be the very same girl who climbed on the wagon and
quenched my thirst. What a pleasure to have such a special
guest. I only wish that I could offer you both some tea and
cakes."

I patted her old, freckled hand. "We came to see you,
not to eat. You remind me very much of my Babi."

"What a proud woman she must be. Is she well, your
Babi?"

"I don't know. She is not here with us . . ." I could
not say any more because I felt the tears welling in my
throat.

Henri began to tell his grandmother about his work in
the ghetto and assured her that he was taking good care of
his mother. She smiled as she listened, and then lay back
with her eyes closed, and we left.

The next afternoon when Henri came by, Gari was with
him and asked Mrs. Gerber if Judi could go walking with
us. Our mothers watched in surprised amusement as the
four of us set off. We walked toward the Weisses' old
house, located within the confines of the factory. A
Hungarian policeman guarding the gate to the house allowed us to pass through after making a few sarcastic
comments about young lovers. As we walked past the
house, the sound of German voices reached us through the

open windows and Gari shrugged. We continued until we came to a much smaller house.

"This is where we live now," Gari said.

We went up the porch stairs and Gari told us to sit down on the wooden chairs and wait for him. He entered the house and after a few minutes came out with a pitcher of breakfast tea, a plate of sliced bread, a jar of gooseberry jam, and four cups. Judi and I were shocked and impressed at the extravagance of food as we watched Gari lower the tray onto the porch table, pour the tea, and spread the jam on the bread. Remembering our manners, we carefully nibbled the bread, sipped the bitter herb tea, and talked. Judi used quotes from different authors and important political figures as a commentary on our possible fate. Gari seemed to admire her extensive book knowledge, and they got into an animated discussion.

Henri and I did not participate much in the conversation, but sat quietly and listened. It was the first time that I had ever sat near a young man so grown-up who was interested in me. After a while we stopped listening altogether and sipped our tea, looking into each other's eyes. Then it was time to go, and we walked back to the shed behind Gari and Judi, who were still talking and gesturing.

After this first meeting, we became a foursome. Henri and Gari came by after they had completed their work detail to take Judi and me for a walk. Mother and Mrs. Gerber had decided to permit us to associate with these older boys.

"I think," Mother said to me after the first night of our being together, "that you know how to behave like a nice girl." I replied, "Certainly," even though I wasn't quite sure what she meant.

Judi and Gari exchanged books and ideas while Henri and I simply enjoyed being together. One day Judi surprised me by saying, "You're so lucky to be at the stage of holding hands. I think that the war will be over before Gari gets the courage to hold mine. He is so shy."

"Shy!" I exclaimed. That description did not fit the Gari I knew.

"The worst part of it," Judi continued, ignoring my

comment, "is that he really cares for me. But if I make the first move, I'll hurt his feelings."

"There you go again, making guesses. You read too much!"

One evening, as Henri and I walked holding hands a slight distance behind Judi and Gari, I asked Henri if he thought Gari was shy.

"No more so than your friend, Judi. If she would only stop talking and be natural, and he could see that she is just a girl, it would be easier for both of them."

I don't know which one of them stopped talking first, but later that evening, as we sat on Gari's porch, I realized that Henri and I were talking and that Gari and Judi were quiet. The sky was cloudy, and we sat in the shadows of dusk. Gari had his arm around Judi's shoulder. A sudden gust of wind carried the German voices toward us, and I shuddered. Mistaking my shudder for a shiver at the chilly wind, Henri took off his jacket and put it around my shoulders.

When the factory whistle that used to signal the end of the workday blew to mark the beginning of curfew, we got up reluctantly to walk back. Gari and Judi led off, walking a few paces ahead of us. Henri pulled me close and locked me in his arms. This time I shuddered from a new emotion that moved like a current through my body. Henri released me and held my face in both his palms for a moment, kissing my lips briefly in a gentle caress. I did not know where I was until we had walked past the German voices in the big house and the Hungarian policeman at the gate.

By this time we had been in the ghetto over a week, and Mother's spirits had begun to show signs of weakening. Although she still tried to help wherever she was needed, she saw that her efforts to demand human treatment from the Germans were futile. She no longer chased after Mr. Shuster with requests and complaints from the inhabitants of shed number 6. She also had to accept the fact that reasoning with the women to keep up appearances at all costs was useless. These people were hungry, frightened, and exhausted. The spring rains kept the earth underneath them damp, and almost all of them suffered from colds and rheumatism. Their bodies were constantly wet despite the thin layers of bedding they had. Mother realized that her demands to keep up appearances might be adding to their misery and discomfort. Over the last few afternoons I noticed that she frequently read from her book on the theater, the only book she had brought from home. Mrs. Gerber was always tired and napped a lot. Judi said that was her way of escaping the reality of the ghetto.

But on this evening of my first kiss, as Judi and I came into the shed, we heard our mothers absorbed in conversation. We stood outside the tent and listened.

"The only reason the theater is better than ordinary life is the rehearsals," Mother was saying. "Take the incident of Lilli's being deported."

Through the sheet in the dim barracks light we saw Mrs. Gerber's silhouette shrug in submission as if to say, "That scene again."

"Now listen, Charlotte," Mother continued, "hear me out just one more time. You know how I have kept going over it in my mind, wishing that I had acted differently. That I would have kept Manci with me no matter what Lilli said. That I should have convinced Lajos to leave Manci with me. If there had been a rehearsal, and I could have seen that half hour acted out with all the mistakes I made, then when the real performance came, I would have been able to be the grandmother, the matriarch, and I would have played my part properly, unafraid that Lilli might resent me. I would have been confident enough to enact my will, because I would have known that later, when Lilli had a chance to reflect on it, she would have understood that I was concerned only with the well-being of the child, not with dominating her. And I also could have made Lajos show his real strength in action. After all, his very fate had come from being reported for taking a stand and speaking out against Hungarian officers. Yes, Charlotte, if we were given a preview of life's moments of crisis, a chance to think instead of having to act in haste, we would not have to go through life blaming ourselves for not having acted properly. That is the big difference between life and the theater. Rehearsals."

"You do pretty well with life as it is," we heard Mrs. Gerber reply. "Certainly a lot better than the rest of us. You will have to let go of that one failure in your life. And you have no reason to give up all hope. Look around you, Rise, look around at the rest of us. Here we are in the ghetto, and you can still make a play out of life."

Mother's arm circled about. "Some play! But we can't give in. They would like nothing better. We must try to beat them at their game." Her voice spoke the words that floated out to us, but she no longer sounded as convinced as she used to. She simply wanted what the rest of the people in the ghetto wanted: to survive with what remained of her family. As Judi and I walked into the enclosure, I could see that Mother's face and body showed signs of wear.

"You girls have been gone for hours," she scolded.

"We were with Gari and Henri," Judi replied.

"Do they know anything?" asked Mrs. Gerber.

"No, we are still waiting for trains."

Mother went over to wash the children's hands and faces with the water she kept for that purpose in a pot. Then she put them to bed on their blanket pallets.

The following morning, after breakfast and Iboya's departure, Mother asked me to stay and watch Sandor and Joli while she heated some water so that she could wash my hair. For the first time in the eight days of our stay, I took a good look at the children. They had grown thin and pale; their energy in play had greatly diminished.

"Do you want to play house and I'll be the daddy?" Sandor asked Joli, taking his shovel and pail to dig in the corner of the tent.

"If you want to," Joli replied without real interest.

"I'll be the mommy," I said, hoping to spark up their mood. They both smiled instantly.

"Will you cook the dinner?" asked Joli coyly. She picked up some small stones from the damp ground and handed them to me. "This will be the meat for soup," she said.

Sandor handed me the pail and shovel. "I'm the daddy,

so I have to go to the army, but I'll be home for dinner."
He ducked outside the tent.

"I'm the baby, so I'll play with my doll." Joli cradled
the worn doll in her pale, mud-stained arms. I remembered
how the doll looked when Lilli had brought it home from
Prague, shining new with long blond hair, painted clay
face, soft pink dress, and patent-leather shoes. Now the
hair was matted and dirty, the face cracked and chipped,
the pink dress soiled and torn, the patent-leather shoes
missing. But Joli did not seem to notice. She spread out a
dirty dish towel and wrapped the doll in it, picked her up
again, and continued to rock her. I mixed some dust with
the rocks and stirred it.

"You did not put in salt and pepper." Joli put down the
doll and pinched at the loose dirt, sprinkling it into the
pail. Then she pinched and sprinkled again. "Now you stir
it all up," she said to me.

Sandor came through the sheet wall by lifting one corner. "Daddy is home from the army. Is the dinner ready?"
He puffed out his chest and goose-stepped, imitating not
our father but the German guards. A chill ran through my
body. I thought of Mother, and what she had said: "I am
going to heat some water and wash your hair."

I told Sandor and Joli, "You stay here and don't move.
I'm going to see Mother and I'll be right back." I walked
outside to the end of the barracks and saw that Mother had
built a stand of stones on top of some twigs in a small pit
and had started a fire. The pot of water sat on the stones,
and she was on her knees, blowing at the sparking twigs.

"Anyuka," I said, touching her shoulder, "you are
going to get into trouble."

"Just go and find Mr. Shuster and see if he can spare a
match. I've got one more, but these sticks are wet and
won't burn. Don't tell him why I want it."

By the time I found Mr. Shuster and came back with the
one match he had grudgingly given me, Mother had succeeded in lighting the fire. She stood up, her face streaked
with soot.

A Hungarian policeman noticed us and came over. "What
are you cooking?" he demanded in a gruff tone.

"Just heating some water to wash my children," Mother answered, keeping her voice even. He reached toward the fire with his club as Mother said, in the same even tone, "Surely you would not deny a mother the right to wash her children."

"Fires are not permitted," he replied brusquely. Mother put herself between the fire and the policeman. "If it were your mother heating water to wash you, would you destroy the fire? What harm is there in trying to keep clean? That water will be warm soon, and I'll put the fire out, I promise you. Nobody else cares about what I am doing. Please be generous, young man."

The policeman, not much older than Henri, looked up at Mother's soot-lined face and bowed his head. "I'll be back in ten minutes. If your fire is not out by then, I'll put it out!"

"Thank you, officer." Mother's even tone did not waver. "You are a kind and generous man." He walked away, and Mother placed the rest of the twigs she had gathered on the fire.

"You go back to the children now," she said to me, "and get out the soap and towels. I'll be along in a minute. We will have to move quickly—this water won't stay warm very long."

When she got back, carrying the pot of water, I had the soap and towels ready. She divided the water to save some for a rinse and covered that pot with a towel to keep it from cooling. I bent over, and she poured the water over my head and rubbed the soap over my scalp. I felt her determined fingers work through my hair. After she finished my hair, she helped me wash my neck, arms, and legs. Then she proceeded to scrub Sandor and Joli as well. Again I was grateful for the sheet walls that provided some privacy.

Afterward she took us outside into the sunlight to dry our hair, and pulled a pair of big shears from her apron pocket.

"If I cut some of your hair, it will be easier to take care of," she said to me. I wanted to protest, but looking up at her concerned face, I could understand that she had to do it, so I sat down on the ground, and she dropped to her knees behind me.

I bit my lips and listened to the squeaking sound of the shears as they clipped away my damp hair. Each strand on the ground measured ten centimeters. How long will it take to grow back, I wondered. I looked around. People were passing by, but no one took any special interest in what we were doing.

Mother took great care with the haircutting. After she finished, she combed it all through several times, then got up and told me to stand up. She stepped away to look at her handiwork, her brows furrowed in concentration. She pulled a small hand mirror from her apron pocket and gave it to me.

"Take a look. I think this length suits your face. It makes you look more grown-up, don't you think?" She stood and waited eagerly for my approval.

I relaxed my teeth and tasted blood. I ran my tongue over a cut in my lower lip. Looking into the mirror, I saw that my hair, half dry by now, was cut to chin length. All the ends curled up in a natural wave, framing my face and making my eyes larger than I was used to seeing them.

"I like it," I said to Mother. "I think Judi will like it, too. It is more like what she calls 'modern.' "

"You have a tough critic in your friend, 'Little Miss Budapesti.' "

"That is a funny name to call Judi, but it fits her."

"Oh, Piri, you look so stylish with your modern haircut," Mother exclaimed, mimicking Judi's flamboyant way of speaking. Though I resented her making fun of my friend, I did have to laugh as she imitated Judi's voice and gestures almost perfectly.

We were still laughing when the young policeman returned to check on the fire; he had given us almost an hour. Stopping a few paces away from us, he listened to our subsiding giggles with a curious interest.

"Wouldn't you like to see my daughter's new haircut?" Mother's voice invited. "Do you think I did a good job?" The policeman started to move toward us and then hesitated.

"I came to make sure you put the fire out. And you will

have to get rid of all that hair," he said loudly from where he stood.

"I will dispose of the hair. And thank you again for letting me heat the water," Mother replied. He gave a small nod of acknowledgment and walked on. Now it was Joli's turn. Mother sat her on the ground and crouched down next to her, shears in hand, but Joli stuffed her long strands of hair inside her blouse.

"No, you can't cut mine," she shouted.

"It won't hurt," promised Mother.

"Don't you want to be stylish like me?" I coaxed, kneeling beside her. Mother looked over at me with an amused glance, and I realized that I, too, was mimicking Judi. We both burst out into a laugh. Joli joined in our laughter and let go of her hair.

"I want mine cut just like Piri's," she announced. Mother cut her hair shorter than mine and pinned it to the side with a red barrette she pulled out of her apron pocket. Joli accepted her new face in the small hand mirror Mother handed her, stood up, and ran over to Sandor to show him her new self.

Mother and I had been right. Judi did think my new appearance more fashionable. "Now you look like my friends in Budapest," she said, surveying me appreciatively when we had all gathered in the tent that afternoon. "Your mother did a fine job."

"Do you think Henri will like it?" I asked Judi nervously.

"He should," she answered. "It makes you look older, more sophisticated."

That evening, when Henri and Gari came to call for us, I watched Henri's eyes as he first noticed the big change. After the initial surprise, he smiled broadly.

"You cut your hair. You look very different."

"She looks more sophisticated," Judi suggested. "More like a Budapesti than a small-town girl. Go ahead, tell her you like it."

"I do," Henri answered. "But I also like small-town girls."

Judi walked away with an air of impatience and Gari followed her. Henri and I fell in behind them as we began the route of our regular evening walk. Henri had become a very important part of my life, and I looked forward to our times together. Sometimes we forgot about our present ghetto existence and made plans for the future.

"I could talk my parents into letting me continue my schooling in Beregszász or apprentice myself to one of the craftsmen. That way we could keep on seeing each other," he said.

"We could go to the cinema," I volunteered, remembering how I watched the older girls going to the films with their boyfriends. Now I, too, could have a boy to go with.

When we got to Gari's house that evening, Gari's mother and father were not there; they had gone to see some friends in the barracks. Gari asked us to come inside the house for the first time. As we walked into the salon, I noticed the nice furniture. "We took it from the big house," Gari explained. But disorder was everywhere as if they were in the midst of moving—clothing and dishes left randomly on tables and chairs.

Gari caught my eyes moving over the disorganized room. "You can see that we are living without a maid. Nobody to pick up after us," he said in a humorously apologetic tone of voice. Shifting some clothing from a table onto a chair, he uncovered a phonograph. "This is all they allowed us to take for music. The piano is still in the big house, even though they don't use it, and having a radio is, of course, against the German rules. I did salvage a few of my records by sneaking them inside some blankets when we moved here. Let's close all the windows, and I'll put one on."

I had a momentary pang as I remembered giving my phonograph to Ica, but it passed and I joined the others in closing the windows and clearing a space in the middle of the room for dancing. I felt nervous about the whole experience. I had danced with other girls in school, and Iboya and I had practiced dancing together, but I had never danced with a boy before.

After the music started, Gari and Judi moved first. I recognized the rhythm of the fox-trot, and the beat seemed to skip inside of me. Gari tapped his foot to the beat and looked over at Judi, who was swaying her whole body to the music. She held out her hands, and Gari took them. Dancing far apart, they kept time as they looked into each other's eyes. Judi's body seemed to absorb the music, to move with it in an easy grace. I had never seen her so relaxed. Gari watched her, smiling, with heightened color in his face.

"Come on, you two," he called to us after the second record started. Judi withdrew her hands from his and slipped into his arms.

"Not with two professionals around like you," said Henri, laughing. He took my hand. "Would you like to try?" he asked softly.

"I've never danced, except with girls, mostly my sisters," I said. But he pulled me up gently, and we eased slowly into following the music. I was just getting a little more confident when Gari's father came through the door. He quickly shut it behind him.

"I can't believe what I am seeing," he said. Gari waved his hand to his father in greeting and went right on dancing, holding Judi, who slowed down her body movement.

"Don't let me stop you," Mr. Weiss said. "I just came to get a blanket. But lower the sound; you don't want them to hear." He motioned with his hand toward the guards' house.

Gari whispered something to Judi, and they both stopped dancing. "Father, would you dance a tango with Judi?" Gari questioned. "She is an excellent dancer."

Mr. Weiss hesitated before replying. "Why not? It has been a long time since I danced. Clear the floor," he joked, rolling down his shirt sleeves and buttoning them.

I had long admired Mr. Weiss's looks. He was, like my father, a large man, but his coloring was very different. In contrast to my father's sandy coarse hair and tanned skin, his hair was deep black, streaked with gray at the temples. His high-cheekboned face had a ruddy quality that gave him, with his big stature, a look of bursting energy. He stood erect and toyed with his trimmed black mustache. Gari changed the record. The slow, precise tango tempo filled the room. Mr. Weiss walked over to Judi and made a low, formal bow.

"May I have this dance?" he asked, holding out his arm. Judi nodded and walked into his outstretched arm, which then bent around her slim back. One of her hands found his shoulder, and she put her other hand into his. She looked frail against his bulk, but they glided evenly across the wood floor. He held her firmly as he bent her body slightly backwards. She tilted her head up to look right into his face. They both seemed to concentrate as much on their pose as on their steps.

Gari, standing with his back to the door, watched the dancers in awe. Henri and I, now seated on the sofa, stared in amazement. I could not believe Judi's ability and composure. Her body, usually restless and gawky, was fluid and graceful. How had she managed to hide all this from me? I wondered. When the music stopped, Mr. Weiss bowed deeply and escorted Judi back to Gari.

"Where did you learn to dance like that, young lady?" Mr. Weiss asked her.

Judi, her shyness returned, blushed deeply. "My father taught me. I used to dance with his friends when we had parties at home in Budapest."

Mr. Weiss smiled at her. "Let us hope that you will soon be back there again, dancing, and not only with your father and other old men." Then he picked up a blanket from a corner, told us to continue our dancing until curfew, and left.

After he had gone, Judi exclaimed to Gari, "I knew that your father would be a marvelous dancer." I both envied Judi and felt sorry for her—she had given up so much because of the war.

21

Each night now when we returned to our ghetto quarters we found Mrs. Gerber sitting with Mother in our tent. She left our cubicle only to sleep. "It is so cozy in here," I heard her say to Mother one morning as she came in. I was shocked by her words. I could barely wait each morning for the end of the ordeal of rolling our blankets and swallowing the lukewarm tea and the stale bread so that I could leave the tent. I found it very depressing.

Mother had made hangers out of sticks wound around with strips cut from a sheet, on which to hang our clothes. The hangers rested on a nail in the beam. No longer as careful about herself, she was still determined to keep us clean. She brushed and inspected my hair every morning. I changed my blouse every second day; she rinsed out our clothes in cold water and spread them out on the grass to dry in the sun. Not to let our appearance slide was her obsession. "As long as you are clean, you won't get sick," she preached.

One morning I left the tent to find the children playing outside. Pali and Carla had joined them. I overheard Sandor say to Pali, "I'll be a German inspector, and we'll pretend that I came to look at your space. I'll be mad and call you *Schwein*; that means 'pig.' " "No," cried Carla, standing nearby, and she ran across to her mother, who was sitting alone in her space.

Carla's mother seldom joined Mother and Mrs. Gerber, who continuously talked about the theater, reminisced about their husbands and their prewar lives, and exchanged recipes for their favorite dishes. I couldn't understand how they could talk about food when they were so hungry. Frequently they visited with other women in the shed, trying to help them cope with the problems of survival. Mr. Shuster stopped by occasionally with some new rumors about the war. All the political news that they could get, he said, seemed to indicate that the Russians were winning. "If they'd just hurry up and get here before the trains come to take us away!" was Mother's constant comment.

Toward the end of our second week in the ghetto, I asked Henri to take me again to see his grandmother in the infirmary. As we came through the door, we saw Mr. Weiss speaking to a group of men near the doctor's partition. They called Henri to join them.

"You go talk to my grandmother. I'll join you in a minute," he told me.

When Henri joined me at his grandmother's bedside, he seemed perturbed and abrupt. "I must get back to the gate," he said after greeting his grandmother. "I'll see you later if I can," and he went off, half running.

I stayed with his grandmother awhile longer, then left, and as I neared our shed, I saw six men walking along the path from the direction of the gate. Henri and Gari walked alongside them, and they were all deeply engaged in conversation. With dismay, I recognized one of the men as Mr. Hirsch from the Juden Bureau. When I told Mother about it, she looked frightened.

"So they are bringing them in, too. It must be all over out there. The Germans have no need of them any more." She spoke in the loudest tone of voice I had heard her use since we had come to the ghetto. Mrs. Gerber came in to see what we were talking about.

"They must have finished cleaning out the city," Mother concluded as she told Mrs. Gerber what had happened.

"Or the trains are finally coming," Mrs. Gerber countered.

"It is all the same." Mother turned to the little ones and then, turning back to me, asked, "Where is Iboya working today?"

"In the kitchen."

"Go see if she knows anything, and don't let anyone hear you talk."

As I walked toward the kitchen, I spotted another group of men being led in. When they came closer, I recognized Mr. Schwartz from the fish store; I called, *"Szervusz,"* and Mr. Schwartz tried to break away from the group, but the two ghetto police made him go back.

"I'll see you later," I called.

"How is your mother? Give her my greeting," he called back, waving his one arm.

People now gathered at the shed entrance and stared at the new arrivals, their faces mirroring their fear as their eyes questioned the significance of the presence of these leaders in the ghetto. I heard one old man say to a woman next to him, "If they are bringing in the specially privileged, it must be the beginning of the end."

As I neared the kitchen, I saw Iboya standing at the entrance talking to a young man. I realized, with great surprise, that it was Shafar, Iboya's friend from the Zionist meetings.

"You remember Shafar?" Iboya asked as I walked up to them.

"Yes, he wrote you all those letters from Budapest." Their serious faces relaxed and they both laughed.

"You just arrived with the others?" I asked him.

"Yes," he answered briefly, offering no explanations.

I turned to Iboya. "Mother sent me to ask you what is happening, why all these men are suddenly being brought into the ghetto. She is very worried about this new development."

"I can't talk now," Iboya answered. "I have to go back into the kitchen."

Shafar bent over and kissed her forehead, and she left us standing there. "I'll go and talk to your mother," he said, putting an arm around my shoulder, "but first I have to stop back at the infirmary." He dropped his arm, and we started to walk. I wanted to ask him why he was in the Beregszász ghetto, but was afraid he would think me forward.

When we arrived, Mr. Weiss and the group of men were still standing by the doctor's partition and talking. Even though they were whispering, their faces were animated. As we approached them, they looked up at Shafar and then questioningly at me.

"Wait for me at the entrance," Shafar said. "I'll be with you in a few minutes."

I went back to the door of the barracks and stood near it, watching the patients. Young ghetto women, Iboya's age and older, wearing the Red Cross arm bands, wove in and out among the cots, trying to make their occupants more comfortable. Again I wished I were old enough to perform a service. Then Shafar joined me, and we walked toward our shed. At the rear entrance we found Judi sitting on the ground, her back against the shed, reading one of her thick books. She jumped up when she saw us and greeted me, never taking her eyes off Shafar.

"This is my best friend, Judi, and this is Joska, Shafar, Iboya's friend," I said. "Shafar has come with me to speak to Mother," I explained to Judi, and all three of us entered the shed.

We walked into the tent. Mother and Mrs. Gerber, sitting and talking as usual, looked up, startled by Shafar's presence.

"You remember Shafar," I said to Mother.

He bowed politely and kissed each woman's hand in turn. Inside the tent, this customary gesture of good manners seemed exaggerated and out of place.

"I hoped not to see you in this place," Mother said to him. "I thought that because of your job you would be spared."

"I am afraid no one will be spared. They are rounding up those who have only one Jewish parent, even those who have been baptized, and God only knows where they will stop."

Mother asked if by any chance Shafar might have heard from Etu before leaving Budapest. He replied that he had heard nothing for the last month or so, but he added that this could be a good sign. The last time he had seen Etu, she was confident about obtaining Christian papers through some of her school friends. "That might very well be the reason she stopped coming around to see me," Shafar concluded.

"Let's hope so," Mother said wistfully.

Mrs. Gerber began to question Shafar about conditions in Budapest: "Were the Jews there also being rounded up? What was their reaction to what was happening to the Jews in other parts of Hungary? Are conditions better in Budapest than in Beregszász?"

Shafar replied to the questions patiently, but his answers all had a similar sound. Conditions for the Jews were the same everywhere, and the rest of the people took no interest because of their own fears and their own problems of survival.

Judi and I walked away and out of the shed, leaving

Shafar and our mothers to their discussions. I told Judi that I had seen Gari's father talking with the other men in the infirmary. "They looked upset over the new developments."

"You mean about the arrival of these men."

"Yes, but I think there is something more. They seemed secretive. They did not want me to hear when they spoke to Shafar. Henri knows whatever it is."

"Did you see Gari there?"

"No. But when I went to the infirmary before with Henri, he said to tell you that Gari was occupied and would see you when he could."

"What about this friend of Iboya's? Who is he and does he know anything?"

"He must, because he talked with the men."

I then went on to tell Judi that Iboya had met Shafar at the Zionist Club, that he had gone to Budapest to work in a munitions factory because he could not serve in the army, and that he and Iboya had corresponded. "I don't know why he is here," I concluded.

Then Shafar emerged from the shed. Judi and I fell into step with him as he started walking in the direction of the infirmary.

"What is going on?" Judi demanded before I could ask Shafar why he was in this ghetto instead of in one with Budapest Jews. "Are we finally going to leave this lovely place?" asked Judi sarcastically, waving her arm in the direction of the sheds and the latrine.

"We don't know for sure," Shafar answered her, "but the arrival of the trains seems imminent, in a day or two." He looked into the shed entrances as we passed by and shook his head in sympathy.

"You think it will be worse than this?" Judi asked in a quavering voice.

"It will be Germany. That is bad enough." We had reached the infirmary, and Shafar bowed slightly to us, then went inside, leaving us to wonder what was going on among the men inside.

"He is very handsome," said Judi. "The only man here in his twenties, I think," she continued. I nodded absently in agreement, thinking Judi's comment, in the light of our present situation, somewhat strange. Still, I had to admit to myself it was true. And I was still annoyed with myself for not having asked Shafar why he was in the Beregszász ghetto.

After supper, Mr. Hirsch came to see us. Mother was not overly friendly at first.

"So they got you in here too," she said.

"We never doubted for a moment that they would put us here eventually," he answered her. "All we gained was two weeks of time for our cooperation in helping them organize things. And in those two weeks we were able to send in a lot of supplies."

"You watch the children," said Mother. "I am going to walk a ways with Mr. Hirsch."

Judi looked at her watch, frowned, and left the tent. Knowing that she was expecting Gari and Henri to appear, I followed her after Mother returned, but stopped when I saw Mr. Schwartz, carrying a paper bag, walking toward our shed. He seemed older and slower-moving. I ran to greet him, and as he stretched his one arm over my shoulders in a hug, I noticed that he no longer smelled of fish. In fact, he almost did not even look like the same Mr. Schwartz. His clothes hung loosely around him, making him look shabby. He handed me the bag as we walked toward our place in the shed.

"Here, Piri, you share these with the family. Your mother and the children are feeling well, I hope?"

"Yes, Mr. Schwartz, we are all well," I answered. Coming to our tent, I held up a corner of the bedspread to usher a surprised Mr. Schwartz inside. Mother was just as surprised and happy to see him. She jumped up and hugged him. Then she stepped back. "You look worn out," she said. "Sit down." And she pointed to one of the bundles. He seated himself slowly and she sat down beside him. "Have you been sick?" she asked.

"I'm not sick," he answered, "just idle. After they closed my store, I tried to be of help at the Juden Bureau, but since I don't speak German, there was little I could do. It is hard to do nothing with so much going on."

"I understand," she said. "We've been sitting here, too, for almost two weeks now."

Mr. Schwartz looked about. "Why did you make this tent arrangement?" he asked.

"Just for some privacy."

I handed Mother the paper bag.

"Did you bring us a fish?" she asked, and they both chuckled with melancholy.

"They let us use the remainder of our bread coupons before they took us, and this was all that was left in the bakery."

Sandor and Joli came from their corner to look as Mother opened the bag. She pulled out a sweet roll, split it in half with her fingers, and let the children eat from her hands, since theirs were covered with the dirt they were playing in. Mr. Schwartz watched Sandor and Joli devour their halves.

"Not a common treat," Mother explained. "We'll save the rest for tomorrow's breakfast to celebrate Iboya's birthday."

Sandor and Joli walked over to Mr. Schwartz and kissed his prickly cheek to express their gratitude. With his one arm he encircled them both and bent forward to kiss them. They giggled and ran back to their play. Mr. Schwartz stood up and said that he had to leave. Mother walked him to the end of the shed. Standing outside the tent, I watched them and the many curious eyes that followed Mother and the one-armed man.

Mother came back, and Mrs. Gerber joined her inside the tent.

"So many visitors in one day," Mother said.

"Did they tell you anything?" Mrs. Gerber asked.

"Mr. Schwartz said that Beregszász is like a ghost town. People don't leave their houses unless they have to."

At that moment, Judi, who had been pacing in and out of the shed for the last hour, came into the tent and whispered to me that she had just seen Henri and Gari crossing the road from the infirmary. They appeared a few minutes later and greeted our mothers, but they seemed preoccupied and upset.

The four of us left the tent, and as soon as we were outside the shed, Gari, noticing the hurt look on Judi's face, apologized for being so late.

"Please," she said to Gari in an urgent voice, her hands reaching for his shoulders, "please tell us what is going on in the infirmary."

Gari looked at Henri. Henri nodded and whispered, "Yes, we can tell them, but not here. We might be overheard."

"Let's go to your house," suggested Judi to Gari.

As we neared the house, we saw Mr. Weiss standing on the porch, looking off into the distance. He was deep in thought, and our arrival startled him. He greeted us with restraint, pulled out his pocket watch to look at the time, and walked into the house.

Then Gari began to speak in a soft voice. "We had formed an underground group and were considering an uprising. Now that the men have come they want to join us. They have no better idea than we did of what plan might work, but most of them feel that we should take some kind of action. They have helped us to smuggle in some guns and ammunition, and they know better than we do how the Germans have organized the city. So far, we have been exchanging ideas."

Judi and I listened in shocked but fascinated silence as Gari continued, "They worked with the Germans. They realize that the Germans can't be trusted, and we don't believe anything they say about the better conditions in the labor camps. The men are determined to do something, even if it only shows them that we are not a pack of cowards. We know as well as they do that we can't keep them from eventually going through with their plans, but we feel the need to act."

"Who are some of the youth workers in the underground?" I asked, knowing that both of them, Henri and Gari, were certainly a part of it.

"Most of the ghetto workers," Gari replied.

"How long have these discussions been going on?" Judi asked.

"We have been talking about forming some kind of a resistance since they rounded us up. But we did not have anything to fight with," Henri said, his face and tone stern.

"And now what do you have?" I asked.

"A few Hungarian rifles, several rounds of ammunition, and some dynamite."

"How did you get it?"

"Some of the guns we managed to buy from the Hungarian peasants on the outside, and they were smuggled in. The buying is not as difficult as getting them in here and hidden away. The German searches are very thorough, because they are looking precisely for such things as guns. Your sister's friend, Shafar, is the one who did most of the work in getting the guns," confessed Gari. "I just took in the last 'shipment' about two hours ago."

"In broad daylight!" exclaimed Judi, alarmed.

"There is no other way to do it," Gari laughed, pleased at her concern.

"My God," said Judi, "you are going to get yourself killed."

Just then the whistle sounded the beginning of curfew, and we all automatically stood up. Mr. Weiss appeared at the door. "Take the girls back to their shed and come right back here. You have done enough for one day," he said to Gari.

After we had passed through the gate, I took Henri's arm and held on to it tightly. "What will you do with all that stuff?" I asked him.

"No two people can agree on any one plan. In a way, it is futile to attempt anything. We are such a small handful of men. Even to deal only with the Germans in the ghetto, we would be outnumbered ten to one, and the rest of their battalion is in the city—a phone call away—a whole army with tanks and machine guns. It's not ourselves we are mainly concerned with, but what will happen to the others, the women and children. Whatever plan we finally decide upon, it won't get us very far."

"Then why do anything?" I pleaded.

"Because a man just can't stand by and let his family suffer without making some kind of an attempt to protect them. Some of the old men say that it is safer to do nothing, that we'll only make things worse if we do anything. But the rest of us feel that any action is better than none at all."

"How do you feel about it?" I questioned.

"I really don't know, Piri. I feel that even if we could blow up the trains as they came in, it would only be a matter of days before more trains come. And who knows what the crazy Germans would do in retaliation in the meantime."

At that point, Gari and Judi caught up to us. Gari had listened to Henri's last words and cut in before Henri had really finished saying what he wanted to say. "But even if we don't accomplish anything more than a delay, it might be worth it. From what the men who just came in are saying, the whole war might be over in a matter of weeks, and the Russians could be here any day."

"But," said Henri, "even if it is true that the Russians will be here in a matter of days, still in those few remaining days God knows what the Germans could do if they got angry enough! And the people in the infirmary might get the worst. They are all too sick to hold out against any further deprivations."

I knew that Henri was thinking of his grandmother, and he and Gari became involved in a heated discussion despite our presence. We parted abruptly as a Hungarian policeman came up to us and said gruffly, "Kiss them and go on your way. It is past curfew time."

Gari and Henri smiled to pretend that the policeman's warning was friendly advice to comrades; then they gave us a kiss on the cheek, turned, and walked on, whistling one of the songs I had written lyrics to. Each of us hiding her fear from the other, Judi and I walked quietly to the shed. Later, lying on my pallet in the tent, I could not fall asleep and heard Judi tossing and turning on the other side of the sheet wall.

*   *   *

The next morning, as breakfast came, Mother told me to ask the Gerbers to come into our tent right after they picked up their tea and slice of stale bread. When we had all gathered, Mother took out the bag of rolls Mr. Schwartz had brought and gave us each a half in celebration, she said, of Iboya's birthday. "Today is May I. Iboya is sixteen years old." Iboya blushed, but looked pleased and thanked Mother. Then she turned to leave.

"A moment, Iboya," said Mrs. Gerber suddenly. "I would like also to do something for your birthday. It will do us all good. Can you be back before they bring supper?"

"I'll try," she said, as she slipped out of the tent.

As soon as we could get away from our mothers, Judi and I walked around the allowed area outside the sheds and talked very softly of nothing else but the danger that our friends were now involved in, a danger that involved us all.

Judi decided that we all had no future, no matter what the men decided to do. "If they decide to take action, it will be disastrous for all of us, but most especially for them. Yet they wouldn't be considering such a futile plan if they felt that our going to Germany wasn't also hopeless."

"Anything they could possibly do will only backfire. So I hope they don't do anything," I said. "I'd rather take my chances on going to Germany and working in their factories. Mother said that at the very least they will have to feed us because in order to work, you have to eat."

"Food is not everything," Judi retorted and went on, "I'm getting to the point where I don't even get hungry. I wish I were a man. At least they can make plans. They don't sit around doing nothing like our mothers, like us."

"But even if we were men, Judi," I said, "we are only thirteen years old."

"Age is not everything, either," she countered. "Personally, I feel a lot older than thirteen, and I don't want to be separated from Gari. Last night he told me that the youth police are staying to help until all of us have been transported and they will be the last to leave here. We might only have a day or two together left, and I am not ready to part."

As Judi finished speaking, I thought about being separated from Henri, and I felt sad, too. "Let us make a pact," Judi said, "and promise that we will act like women if the two of them come by for us this evening. It would be nice if we could dance together one more time. But whatever happens, let's act grown-up. We might not have another chance."

"I think I'll go back to the tent and write a poem for Iboya's birthday," I said, changing the subject.

"Good idea. I think I will look among my books for one to give her," said Judi.

That afternoon we were gathered in the tent for Iboya's second birthday party. Shafar walked her back from the kitchen at 4 p.m. He had given her his school ring as a present, and he had also managed to trade some cigarettes with one of the Hungarian guards for a large loaf of bread. Mother accepted the bread, cut it into nine wedges, and passed the pieces to us. Mrs. Gerber held her gift in her hand, and before giving it to Iboya, she made a presentation speech.

"This is for the brave and wonderful young woman with the promise that, when the war is over, I'm going to make you a real party, the kind you deserve, at my father's house in Budapest, where we'll have champagne, music, and the proper presents."

Iboya then took the brown paper bag, opened it, and pulled out Mrs. Gerber's white silk embroidered shawl. She put it over her shoulders and twirled around, brushing us with the long, silk fringes as she turned. We stood there admiring her, and then took our turns in kissing her and wishing her a happy birthday. I gave her the poem I had written, and Judi gave her a thick book. Shafar left, but said that he would return later.

And so that evening three young men came to call after we had finished eating our supper, and all three of them were freshly shaved. Mother's face lit up when she looked at them. They bowed to her in greeting and said their "Good evening," and then the six of us left the tent. Iboya wore her new shawl carefully draped over her shoulders. When we got to the gate surrounding the Weiss residences, the guards questioned the presence of Shafar and Iboya. Shafar brought two packages of cigarettes out of his breast pocket and gave one to each guard, and they waved us in.

Mr. Weiss was standing on the porch, and he asked the six of us to come into the house. Inside, in the salon, Mrs. Weiss, wearing an elaborate dressing gown, was stirring a pitcher filled with a raspberry drink. She welcomed us as though we were her very special friends, and then explained, "I still had some syrup left, so I mixed a punch for the occasion of Iboya's birthday, and I have some jam left as well. Not an elegant party, but the best I could manage under the circumstances."

I glanced at Iboya, thinking that news travels fast in the ghetto. Mr. Weiss sliced up some bread and cut it into small pieces; then he brought out some glasses and Mrs. Weiss poured a drink for each of us.

Mr. Weiss raised his glass. "Let us all pretend that this is champagne. A toast to Iboya and to a future of freedom where young love can flourish." As we clinked our glasses, I made my own silent toast—like the one Mother had made at the seder—"Next year may we all be together in Komjaty." As we drank the punch and savored small bites of bread spread with emerald-green gooseberry jam, Mr. and Mrs. Weiss admired the ring Shafar had given Iboya and the silk shawl from Mrs. Gerber. After we finished eating, Mr. Weiss took Henri, Gari, and Shafar with him into the other room and closed the door.

"Men," said Mrs. Weiss with annoyance. "They have to have their little secrets of war and games."

I watched Iboya admiring Mrs. Weiss' gestures, and I realized that Gari's mother was beautiful and graceful. Her dressing gown swirling gently about her, she collected the glasses and floated across the room to set them down on a small table against the wall. Then she sat down elegantly on the sofa next to Iboya and began to speak to her.

"I've heard that your Shafar is quite a man. He came to Beregszász, I understand, after running from Budapest, and turned himself in. Not many have the courage to walk into the German headquarters and say, 'I'm ready to go to the ghetto.' I guess he made them think that he was too scared to keep on running. Smart boy. Where did you meet him?''

I was glad to have my question about Shafar's appearance in the Beregszász ghetto answered at last. Iboya was saying that she had met Shafar at the Zionist Club before he left for Budapest.

''He is so impressive,'' Mrs. Weiss said, ''and brave, too. I'm sure his job in Budapest was just a front for other things. Had I known that there were men of his caliber in that club, I might have joined it myself.'' She chuckled, to make a joke of her statement, but I wondered how much of a joke it really was.

The atmosphere in the salon grew heavy; none of us dared to speak for fear of saying the wrong thing. Mrs. Weiss turned her attention to Judi.

''And you, my dear, I have heard, are an excellent dancer.''

''Thank you. In Budapest we used to have many parties,'' Judi managed to say.

''Oh yes,'' said Mrs. Weiss, ''I know what you mean. We used to have many parties, too, in the big house. How long ago it all seems. Soon we won't remember.'' Mrs. Weiss walked over to the phonograph, put a record on, and cranked the handle. A waltz melody drifted over the room. She held up her arms to an imaginary partner and waited for the beat; then she started to circle, weaving her way in and out between the tables and chairs. The door to the other room opened, and the men came into the salon. They looked at Mrs. Weiss gliding about, first with surprise, then with amusement.

She danced over to Shafar and stretched her arms out to him. He hesitated and then, encircling her waist with his right arm, said, ''Well, I'll try, but this sort of thing is not my line.''

''It is easy,'' she said, looking down at their feet. ''Count the beats as you step—one, two, three; one, two, three.'' They circled away, and Mr. Weiss checked to make sure that the windows were closed. After moving some chairs out of the center of the room, he came over to

Iboya and asked her to dance. Her face flushed to match the embroidered roses in her shawl, but she got up and moved gracefully into Mr. Weiss's outstretched arm. Her body remained stiff, but her feet easily followed.

"And where did you learn to waltz, Iboya?" Shafar asked her after the music had stopped.

"My brother-in-law, Lajos, taught me."

Gari cranked up the phonograph again, turned the record, and asked Judi to dance. They had the floor all to themselves as the rest of us stood and watched. Judi's toes hardly touched the ground as Gari and she waltzed round and round. With her skirt billowing out from her tiny waist, she floated past us effortlessly. Mr. Weiss started to applaud, and we all joined in. Then the curfew sounded, and we said our goodbyes and thank-yous to Mr. and Mrs. Weiss. Henri and I led the way through the gate, followed by Iboya and Shafar and then, a little farther back, Gari and Judi. We said our good nights to our escorts in as much privacy as we could each manage.

Henri stood with his back against the shed's beam and pulled me close to his chest. I could hear his heart beating and felt very sad yet very peaceful. We stood that way without moving for a few minutes. Then Henri released me, cradled my face in his hand, and kissed me gently on the lips. He dropped his hands abruptly, turned, and walked away. I went straight into the shed without looking back.

22

The following morning, as soon as we were outside together, Judi told me that she and Gari had kissed good night in an adult fashion with their lips parted. "You must try it, if you get another chance," she said.

Her frankness irritated me even though it aroused my curiosity. But she was right about our not having another chance. As we stood outside the shed, Mr. Shuster passed us on his way in, and we followed him into our tent.

Startled by his gloomy appearance, Mother and Mrs. Gerber gave him all of their attention as he told them that he had just received orders to get us ready for our departure.

"Oh, my God!" Mother cried out. Mrs. Gerber turned white and remained speechless.

"I'm going to post the instructions at the front of the shed, and I'll need some help in getting these women organized. Even though they were expecting it, it will still be a shock to them. I hope you ladies will give me a hand in carrying out these orders."

He had just stepped outside the tent with the four of us behind him when a German officer entered our barracks, with two Hungarian policemen. The officer called loudly in German—*"Achtung!"*—and there was an instantaneous and eerie silence. One of the Hungarian policemen began to speak. "The trains are expected today or tomorrow. You are being taken to work in factories in Germany, where you will be treated well, so there is no cause for alarm. You are to pack up your belongings and address them to Work Camp Number 500, Germany. Print your names and the address carefully; your baggage will be sent to you on the next train. Mr. Shuster will assist you, but you must cooperate fully with these orders." He finished speaking and, in the German way, clicked his heels together and saluted the German officer, who had been glaring at the crowd of hushed women. Then the three of them turned and walked out.

Iboya appeared, running. She was trembling as she came up to us where we stood near the entrance to the shed beside Mr. Shuster, who was nailing up the instructions.

"They have dismissed me," she cried and flung herself into Mother's arms. "We are in the first transport. They are loading us alphabetically."

"Are they dividing us up?" Mrs. Gerber asked with alarm.

"There will be about three or four transports. The youth police and the infirmary will be the last to go."

"I don't want to go without you," Mrs. Gerber said to Mother and started to cry.

Judi and I looked at each other and our eyes welled with

tears. "Come on," said Judi to me, "let's look for them," and we walked to the back of the shed.

Iboya ran after us. "Don't go looking for them," she said as she caught up with us. "They are in a meeting. If they have a chance, they will come here. Otherwise, last night was a farewell. We have to help these women get themselves together."

I looked around the shed and saw some women starting to gather their children, others poking aimlessly among their bundles. Mr. Shuster had walked down to the back of the shed, and Mrs. Gerber followed him.

"Don't let them separate us," she appealed to him. "Our two families must stay together."

"If it's up to me, I'll keep you together. But I can't promise," he whispered back. She walked over to her space and began to fold up her blankets.

Iboya began to tear down our sheet wall and cut it into small squares.

"Here," she said to Judi and me as we stood there watching her, "pass these squares out among the women and tell them to print their names and 'Work Camp 500' on them and sew them onto their bundles. We have a few extra needles and some thread for those who need it."

At last we had our chance to be helpful. Not only did we distribute the white squares of sheeting, but we also helped the women print their names and the address on the squares before they sewed them onto their bundles. We worked with our ears straining to register any distant sound. After we had finished, Judi and I walked up to the front of the barracks and looked across the fields to the empty tracks. But they were no longer empty; trainmen were working on them.

"It's being readied," Judi commented.

Returning to the barracks, we found people sitting on their bundles, almost as if they expected the train to come right into the shed. Mr. Shuster paced up and down, chewing on his pipe, obviously disturbed by unnatural quiet in shed number 6. Finally he walked outside.

Judi and I followed Mr. Shuster and saw him look across the fields at the workmen on the tracks. We turned our gaze to the infirmary, hoping to see Gari and Henri coming toward us. But the road was empty. Judi noticed Mr. Shuster looking at his watch. "It appears as if you can't wait for the trains to come," she snapped at him.

"If we are going, it might as well be soon," he answered. "What good is this waiting to any of us?"

"I'm in no particular hurry," said Judi with sarcasm.

I decided then to ask Mr. Shuster the question gnawing at me ever since the coming of the trains was announced. Watching all those people following so readily the German orders to leave their lives behind, I couldn't help wondering what would happen if we were not so obedient.

"Mr. Shuster," I asked hesitantly, "what would happen if we refuse to leave when the trains come?"

Mr. Shuster turned toward me, still chewing on his pipe as he weighed my question. Judi spoke up. "She means if we put up a resistance."

He removed the pipe from his mouth and held it, the bowl cupped in his hand, as he spoke. "Girls, the answer is self-evident, but I'll answer it by asking you a question. Why do you think the Hungarian police and the German guards carry rifles with bayonets? I understand how you feel, but I'm afraid we have no choice."

"Man always has an alternative, and a choice," Judi retorted. "It has been demonstrated throughout history in every war."

"Demonstrated, yes, but rarely accomplished. In order to resist, your position has to be comparable to your enemy's. They have an iron army, and we—we don't even have men."

"Many well-known resistance groups were made up of small numbers of people," Judi persisted.

"Look around you, Judi. What do you see?" Mr. Shuster waved his arm about. "A pack of frightened women and children with a few old men scattered among them. Some resistance group we would make."

"We have some young men and also some women who are not afraid," Judi continued to argue.

"To be brave is very honorable. To be foolhardy is very wasteful. I thought I was being brave when I deserted my work group and went to look for my family. But I was picked up before I could find them. Now I am without my comrades as well as without my family.''

To my astonishment, Judi became sympathetic. "I'm really sorry about your bad luck, Mr. Shuster," I heard her say in a deflated voice.

"It is the times. Very bad to be a Jew during depressions. We make such perfect scapegoats.''

"Why?" I asked.

"Because we are a minority, well conditioned to persecution. Sometimes I think that this is our purpose.''

"To be scapegoats? That sounds very unfair," Judi commented. "Especially since we are supposed to be the chosen people.''

"To be chosen is a big responsibility," said Mr. Shuster. "Sometimes God uses us in very strange ways.''

I was confused. It all sounded too complicated to me. "Mr. Shuster," I asked, "what exactly is a scapegoat?''

He stopped poking his thumb into the bowl of his pipe and answered slowly, "In the Bible, when Aaron's sons died, God told Moses to go to Aaron and tell him to lay the sins of the Jews on the head of a sacrificial goat and to send the goat out into the wilderness to carry off all the sins of Israel.''

So that's what Mother meant when they took away Ladybeard, I reflected.

"But these are not our sins," I said, "they are the Germans". Why should we have to carry them?''

"The Germans are twisting God's words and sending us to carry their sins into the wilderness.''

"If this is the way God chooses to use His people, I'd rather not be chosen," said Judi defiantly. "We are what we allow ourselves to be. The whole concept of Judaism is archaic. Both our culture and tradition are cowardly. We obey out of fear, not devotion, and forfeit our freedom. As a consolation we have accepted or invented the belief that we are the chosen people. What an outrageous excuse! I, for one, am not going to be used for such a purpose. I don't even consider myself Jewish.''

Mr. Shuster shrugged his shoulders. "If you come up with a good solution, I would like to hear about it."

"We just might," said Judi, taking my hand and leading me away. She seemed more troubled than angered. "Mr. Shuster is not as simple as I imagined he was. He lets the Germans use him as an errand boy not out of stupidity but because he's given up fighting them. All his fighting energy went into trying to trace his family. And now that he's failed, he has no fighting left in him. So he accepts what has happened as the will of God. Well, that may be his answer, but it isn't mine."

"So what will you do?" I asked, hoping that she wouldn't give in, the way Mr. Shuster already had and the way that my mother was starting to.

I felt sorry for Judi. She had been misled by her liberal upbringing to believe that she did not have to live by restricting rules. She had been taught she was a Hungarian, but now found out she was a Jew. Her false security was crumbling and she had no identity to hold on to.

Her shoulders sagged as her expression grew more concentrated. "I wish I were a man! I wish I were older! I hate to be left out of things!" She spoke harshly and kicked at some pebbles as we walked back to our mothers and the children.

The shed was filled with silent people, sitting on their bundles. Once we were in our space, Mother quickly handed us each a last piece of toast. We chewed on the morsels until they were moist and then swallowed them down through tight throats. Sandor and Joli gathered up their toys, and Mother packed the pails, shovels, and the old spoons, cleaned of their ghetto clay, into a bundle. Iboya took her notebook from her duffel bag and began to draw pictures of animals to amuse the children.

Henri came by before supper. "No sign yet of the trains," he told us. "We doubt that they will come today."

"Would they board us after dark?" Mother asked anxiously.

"No," Henri said, "they wouldn't take the risk of letting some people slip away. If the trains don't come within the next hour, chances are that you won't leave until tomorrow.''

"It will be some night, then,'' Judi said bitterly. "We are all packed. We will have to sleep sitting up; the earth is too cold to lie on. Where is Gari?'' she added, changing the subject.

Iboya put down her notebook and joined us. "Have you seen Shafar?''

"They are both listening for the train. They will be able to hear it two kilometers away.''

"How?'' Mother asked.

Without the hanging sheet walls of our tent around us, I felt exposed, and all eyes and ears seemed to be directed toward us as we crowded around Henri. He answered Mother's question, speaking very softly. "They just have a way of listening.'' Looking at his watch, he then spoke in a normal tone of voice. "No, I don't think the trains will come today. Most likely it will be tomorrow.''

I looked at the people sitting all around us. Their bodies seemed to sag in disappointment, and I could hear fragments of comments: "How shall we sleep?'' "They told us to pack.'' "What about supper?''

Judi and I followed Henri outside, and as soon as there were no people around us, we both asked simultaneously, "What has been decided?''

"We have not reached a decision.''

"Then why are they listening for the trains?'' Judi snapped.

"So that we can have some advance notice,'' Henri answered her in an even voice.

"Could you tell Gari that I would like to see him before curfew?'' Judi asked in a gentler tone.

"I'll tell him,'' said Henri, "but I can't promise you anything.''

Judi took a letter from her pocket and handed it to Henri. "Please take this to him, but tell him not to open it until after we're gone.''

Henri put the letter in his pocket and walked away. We went back to our families in the shed. Mother and Mrs. Gerber were quietly talking; Iboya was again drawing pictures and writing words for the children. Judi and I sat down on our bundles and both of us were suddenly without energy, even to talk to each other.

Shafar and Gari came into the shed shortly after supper and told us that a large reinforcement of German guards had arrived from the city. The night watch force of the ghetto was also being doubled. Gari and Henri were to be stationed at assigned posts alongside the Hungarian police. Judi asked Gari if he could get himself assigned to our barracks.

"I have no influence with the Germans."

"You speak their language and your name still is Weiss," Judi retorted.

"I have some packs of cigarettes left if you think that would help," Shafar offered. Gari took the two packages of cigarettes that Shafar held out and put them in the breast pocket of his shirt. Shafar told Iboya he would try to get back to us, but they now had to go. We watched them until they disappeared from view beyond the back exit of the shed.

The atmosphere in the shed was more depressed than ever. Children, overtired and confused, began to cry. Mother and Mrs. Gerber started to unpack blankets and stopped when they realized that they might not have time to repack them. Mother flattened down a few of the bundles and put Sandor and Joli on top of them.

As the children slept, we all sat up, dozing from time to time, whispering to each other, and above all listening for the train. Mother and Mrs. Gerber began, once again, to reminisce about their lives. We sat listening to them, amazed to discover how little we knew about the girlhoods of our mothers. How surprised we were to hear that their feelings when they were girls had been very much like ours. Mother spoke about our father, the first man she had ever loved. Mrs. Gerber talked about how much she had wanted to be a writer and how she had kept a diary hidden in her drawer. All their secrets and hopes were discussed in the darkness of that night.

For the first time, Iboya even talked to Judi and me about Shafar. She did not think that she would see him again, at least not until the war was over. "We said our real goodbyes last night and promised to wait for each other."

Judi told us what she had written in her letter to Gari. "I asked him not to take chances with his life because I want to meet him again when the war is over and to continue our courtship on an adult level. I want to experience with him all the sensations of a mature romance—all the things I have read about in books. I don't want to be cheated of any of life's promises."

Once again I envied Judi's sophisticated attitude toward romance. Henri and I had simply promised to try to stay in contact with each other from wherever we were sent.

By listening to us and sharing her feelings with us, Iboya had treated us as her equals. But she was two years older than we and restrained in temperament. She did not easily discuss her feelings with anyone. When Judi asked her what it was like to be with a grown-up man, Iboya answered simply, "I don't think age alone decides; individuals and circumstances make the difference."

"But you and Shafar are old enough to get married," Judi persisted. "You can do anything. You don't have to stifle your desires."

I could see that Iboya was slightly annoyed at Judi's persistence, but she answered her patiently. "Shafar is a sensible and reserved man."

"Sensible," Judi hissed in a loud whisper. "Why should we be sensible when nothing around us makes any sense? What if we never see them again? Think of what we'll miss. Won't you be sorry then?"

"I can't read the future," Iboya said, with less patience. "I can only do what I think is best right now."

Suddenly we were aware of a rustling sound around us. We had been so absorbed in our discussion that we had not noticed the dawn beginning to break and the gray light piercing the shadows. Throughout the barracks, people were stirring, standing up from their hunched positions and moaning as they stretched their stiff bodies. Mr. Shuster appeared, making his rounds to see if we had all survived the night; he looked haggard, his eyes sunk into deep hollows.

Iboya, Judi, and I were just walking back from our turns at the latrine when we heard the clacking sound of the train approaching the brick factory. I heard it with all of my being—not as a sound, but as a total experience—and was filled with terror. A tremor shook my body. We tried to run but found ourselves planted in the ground, and as the train pulled into view, we saw that it was not the kind of train we had expected. Instead of the usual passenger cars with windows and seats, it consisted of a long line of rust-colored cars like the ones cows were loaded into. The cars of the train were tall, closed up, with only small openings near the roofs.

When we were finally able to pick up our feet, I ran back to Mother feeling my body grow hot as the sweat poured down my face. She was not in our space. All the people had gone up to the front of the shed to watch the train. I found her in a cluster of women, one of whom said, "So it is true . . . I thought it was just a rumor." But no one had the time to ask what she meant, because the German soldiers had started to push their way through the crowd at the entrance. As I looked at one of them, my eyes first made contact with his black, shiny gun belt, then slowly traveled up his gray uniform, arriving at the ice-blue stony gaze that recognized nothing.

"We are all God's children," Babi used to say, meaning both Jews and Christians. Did she mean Germans, too? I wished that I could ask her. They did not look like anybody's children, and they looked not at us, but through us as if we didn't exist.

With a shock, I realized that I had looked forward to going to Germany the way one anticipates a new adventure. Now I did not want to know anything about the coming adventure.

"*Mach schnell!* Make ready to depart. You can take only what you are carrying on your person. Your belongings will be sent by the next train."

I no longer believed anything they said about us or our things.

"They are not going to separate us!" Mrs. Gerber
whispered in relief.

We all moved empty-handed out of the barracks, merg-
ing with the crowds from the other sheds as we walked
toward the train. The white-arm-banded guards were trying
to organize us into lines of five abreast. The five of
us—Mother, Iboya, Joli, Sandor, and I—held hands as we
walked. Mrs. Gerber, Judi, and Pali were right in front of
us, with Carla and her mother completing their line of
five. I noticed Judi turning her head around as I was
doing, and realized that she was looking for Gari just as I
had been trying to spot Henri. With so many people
everywhere, it was impossible to distinguish one person.
An exodus of families moved through the fields, German
and Hungarian officers walking between them. Nothing
seemed real.

We slowed down, stopped, started to move again, inch-
ing along. Joli began to whimper, and Mother picked her
up. Gari appeared out of the crowd. He tapped Judi on the
shoulder with his stick. She moved out of her line, stood
aside, and took his hand. "Did you read my letter?" she
asked with concern.

"Yes," he answered, "I read it last night. Just a moment, I want to ask Mrs. Davidowitz something." He
turned to Mother.

"Mrs. Davidowitz, I overheard two trainmen talking,
and one mentioned the word 'Auschwitz.' You speak German better than I do. Do you know what it means?"

"No," she answered. "I'll try and ask Mr. Shuster."
He turned back to Judi and they stood talking to each other
until one of the German guards came up and waved Judi
back into line. Gari walked off toward the front of the
lines. I was not sure that I wanted to see Henri right now. I
felt sweaty, light-headed from lack of sleep, and my mind
reeled with fears of the future.

The lines in front of us started to disintegrate, and we
moved forward until we could see a group of German
soldiers stop the line in front of the Gerbers and search the
people, reaching in and under their clothing. Then the
Gerbers were next. One of the soldiers grabbed Judi and

put his hand inside her blouse. Mother put Joli down and clutched Iboya and me to her sides.

"*Nein!* You will not touch my daughters!" she declared in German and repeated in Hungarian, her voice filled with anger and fear.

They laughed at her, and as we came into the first line position, Iboya, Mother, and I were pulled apart by three of the leering Germans. The back of my neck was suddenly in an iron grip, and a coarse, rough hand brushed down my chest and over each of my breasts, bursting the buttons of my blouse. Bending over me so close that I could smell his sausagy breath and see the tobacco stains on his teeth, the soldier reached into my bloomers and felt inside my private parts. I couldn't tell if the stinging in my eyes was more from hurt or shame. He shoved me on. When I looked up toward the train, I saw Henri down the platform, about four meters away, and I quickly turned my head, hoping that he had not seen us being searched. The Gerbers and Carla and her mother had by now boarded the freight car. They stood looking down at us, frightened and silent, Mrs. Gerber with one arm reaching toward Mother. It didn't seem that the car could hold any more people, and we stood still. But the German guard motioned us to climb up. Mr. Shuster and some of the white-arm-banded youths, Gari among them, boosted us up until we stood in the car with our backs tightly squeezed against the others. Mother leaned down and asked Mr. Shuster, "Do you know what 'Auschwitz' means?" But before he could answer, the German guard yelled, "*Achtung! Rein! Rein!*" and Mother pulled her head back just in time to avoid being struck by the door as it closed with a loud metallic clank.

Afterword

Mrs. Davidowitz, Iboya, Piri, Sandor, and Joli arrived in Auschwitz on May 9, 1944. Iboya and Piri were separated from the rest of the family on that day and never saw them again. In September, they were selected to work in the kitchen of the concentration camp at Christianstadt, where the inmates worked in a munitions factory. This accounted for their eventual survival. With the Russians rapidly approaching, the Germans made them leave there in January 1945 and walk to Bergen-Belsen, a journey that lasted until the beginning of March. On April 19, 1945, Field Marshal Montgomery's First Army liberated the camp. In June, Iboya and Piri were taken by the Swedish Red Cross to Sweden, where they began to rebuild their lives. They immigrated to the United States in 1948. Aranka Siegal, the Piri of the story, now lives in New York.